ELIJAH & THE SAT

Reflections on a hairy old
desert prophet
and the benchmarking
of our children's lives

Heather Choate Davis

STEWART PRESS

To Remy
"I know the plans I have for you,
plans to prosper and not to harm you"
(Jeremiah 29:11)

We need an older angel
if we're gonna make it through
One who's been around this block
we're on a time or two

-Kate Campbell

Chapter 1

The story never changes. As it was in 885 BCE so it is today. So it was in 1873, when a bright, eager 16-year old Massachusetts girl set out to conquer the demands of her junior year. Her parents, both staunch advocates of higher education, expected their daughter to go to college—an important college—but that dream came to an abrupt end when Fannie Merrit Farmer had a severe and inexplicable stroke. Her prime young adult years were spent instead confined to a bed where she could do little more than reflect on her daily readings and prayers. Her physical healing was incomplete, but her strength and her spirit and her will to move on with her life returned in full measure and, as it did, she began to cook. Before long, the Farmer family boarding house had earned a reputation throughout New England for its delicious fare. At the age of 30, Fannie enrolled in the Boston Cooking School where she developed her gifts even further. She became the dean of the Boston Cooking School and later opened an institute of her own, Miss Farmer's School of Cookery, where she not only taught and created recipes, but wrote papers on nutrition, sanitation, diet, cooking techniques, household management, and the specific dietary and nutritional needs of convalescents, subjects she was invited to lecture about at the Harvard Medical School. Her greatest legacy, however—one that still impacts every person who picks up a recipe today—is in the area of measurement. It was Fannie Farmer who first recognized that the use of haphazard measuring tools—a teacup or a soup spoon or a few fat fingers—led to less than optimal and sometimes disastrous results. If we wanted to control the outcome of a fine fig pudding, we needed to know the difference between a heaping and level teaspoon, and what constituted a teaspoon in the first place.

For as long as we have recorded history, men and women have sought to bring order and control to the materials of their day through measurement. Ivory yardsticks have been found among the 5000-year old ruins of the Indus Valley civilization. The Ark and the Tabernacle were built to God's specifications in cubits and cords. The Ancient Greeks and Egyptians joined best practices to form a reliable method of weights and measures. Time was contained by Julius Caesar, who helped create the first solar calendar, and then by a string of Europeans who developed, 1100 years later, the hourglass and the town clock. But that's ancient history. We now live in an era where we have total control of our physical realm (well, except for the occasional "Act of God"). We've moved on to measuring the realm of the mind and behavior and the technology that serve them. We have sexy, codified assessments for everything: intelligence, aptitude, risk, odds, and the ever-critical return on investment—or, as it's more commonly referred to, ROI. Still, when it comes to understanding the measure of a life—a life well lived, a life of value, a wonderful life, even—statistics are about as useful as a footnote.

According to the beloved holiday movie of the same name, a wonderful life is one in which you don't get your heart's desire, your dreams are thwarted, you are repeatedly on the brink of financial ruin, and none of it adds up to the life you envisioned. But step back from that ledge, my friend and you'll see that the role you've played has been a blessing to many people and that the universe is infinitely better for you being—well, you. In the season of love and forgiveness, when even rational souls are inclined to light a candle or look longingly at the night sky, we are granted a momentary reprieve from our fact-loving selves; we put down our armor and unclench our fists. No, our lives are not perfect, but we have a warm room to watch a movie in and leftover pie in the fridge and children who probably won't make valedictorian but who nonetheless make us smile and give us hope and sometimes even rub our feet if we ask them nicely. Despite all our shortcomings, life *is* good and we can almost imagine, as the credits role, having the courage to believe in an angel who can point out how misguided we get with our grandiose ideas sometimes. But then vacation ends and—faster than you can say weighted GPA—we pack up our DVDs and our wishful thinking and get back to the business of earning and striving and pushing and forging exceptional kids out of the chaos of our overscheduled days. This is 21st century America, after all. Not even our children have time for fairy tales.

When my son Graham was two and a half, my aunt was the director of an exclusive pre-school program run by an Episcopal church in Beverly Hills. She let us join their weekly toddler group where all of the mothers were a decade or two older than me. Most had older kids, as well— 5- and 8- and even 10-year old kids—some who were already in therapy. No one seemed to be there for religious reasons, no one but the teachers, who I now know had likely prayed each morning before class for an opening in which to plant a seed of light or truth in a willing heart. One day I made the mistake of asking one of them, privately, on the sidelines of circle time, about Death. Specifically, how to talk to young children about Death.

"Well," she said gently, "I suppose it depends on what you believe. For me, personally, I believe that when we die we go to Heaven to be with God and Jesus and all the Saints and angels. And that's not hard to talk to kids about at all."

How nice for you, I thought. Returning to the circle of sophisticated heathens, I realized I was angry in a new, unspoken, unspeakable way. I hated her for that answer. I resented her kindness and her confidence. Despised the possibility that she and others like her could have the last laugh about the most important thing I'd ever endeavored to do in my life. I placed Graham's hands in mine as we circled them around like wheels on a bus and affirmed in my spasming heart that I would do anything to do right by him. Like a g-force drop in a cable-slackened elevator, the first seed gave root to an even more terrifying thought: was it possible, despite all my brilliant, enlightened ideas to the contrary, that the people—*those people*— who believe in God were actually the ones who had the edge when it came to raising kids?

Elijah the Tishbite never had any kids. He was a child of God, a prophet from the town of Tishbe in the region of Gilead in the early part of the 8th century, BCE. He's referred to in Bible study lingo as a "minor prophet" because he takes up so little space in the narrative; his resume is buried in a stack of two sequential books in the Old Testament, neither of which is even named after him. And yet, his days were a relentless stream of singular accomplishments, rare acts of bravado and wit, miraculous moments of healing and provision, stunning seasons of prayer and silence, and divine revelations that poured out from his life in the form of living proof so profound no willing heart could remain untouched by his presence. His story is shared by Jews and Christians and Muslims alike, who recount how, throughout biblical history, every generation that followed would approach potential messiahs to ask breathlessly, "Are you Elijah?" Prophets came and went, saints and kings, rabbis and scholars, judges and warriors, wise and faithful men and women who fleshed out the story of God, but it would be none other than Elijah who would reappear on the mountain top at the

Transfiguration, taking his rightful place beside the two greatest figures in the Judeo-Christian tradition: Moses and Jesus Christ.

Why him? Elijah was not a worldly man. He was not charming or gracious or multi-talented. We have no indication that he was especially attractive or athletic or intelligent. He did not play well with others or mix with the right crowd—in fact, if he'd needed a letter of recommendation to get a meeting with a king, he wouldn't have known a single person to ask. Yet, so great was his impact on the world that today, 3000 years later, the Jewish faithful still hold an empty seat for him at the table in the hopes that he will return.

What did his parents do to raise a son like that? What special secrets did they know about nurturing kids who'd go on to be living legends? The evidence is scant. On the day he was born his mother and father named him Elijah—"my God is the LORD." At first glance, this may seem perfectly ordinary—a nice Jewish name for a nice Jewish boy—but it was a fist-pumping act of pure and defiant faith. Israel was no longer a nation devoted solely to the God who had given them life. Seduced by Jezebel and her blinged-out pantheon, the children of Abraham and Isaac and Jacob had started to forget about the God who had brought them out of slavery and blessed them with fertile land and all the commandments they'd ever need to ensure they'd live long in it and prosper. They'd become dabblers. They wanted their big old-fashioned sea-parting God and their sexy, new palm-reading gods too. In the house of Elijah there was only one God: Yahweh, the covenant name God spoke to Moses. Yahweh comes from the Hebrew word *to be*, and is translated as **"I AM WHO I AM"** or **"I am the One who is"** (Exodus 3:14). In Hebrew scripture it is written as YHWH—in English, LORD. Yahweh. Not one of many. Yahweh. Not interchangeable with whatever bright, shiny new gods come along. Yahweh. The ONE who IS. **"This is my name forever, and this my title for all generations."** (Exodus 3:15). This is what Elijah's parents taught their son—not with flashcards, but with their very lives: Yahweh is the LORD. *Pray. Listen. Obey.*

In our post-everything culture, *obey* has become a four-letter word. Obeying is for wimps. Obeying is for people who didn't do well enough on their SATs to write their own rules. Only the weak and the feeble and the young—well, not even the young anymore—need to obey. Funny, because the root of the word *obey* is from the French verb meaning "to listen, or to give ear to." It was never intended as a militant word, but one of hearing, of understanding. Of getting it. For a world obsessed with staying in constant communication, we aren't really very good listeners. I don't think a year goes by when I'm not faced with some perturbed adult shouting, "You're not listening to me!!!" After I've checked myself carefully to make sure that this is not the case, that I am in fact listening, that I could repeat back both the spirit and the truth of what was conveyed, I realize I am looking at a prime example of what we have come to view as listening. Listening means "I told you what I thought was the right thing to do, and it is so obviously the superior solution that the very fact that you have not reversed your position and implemented mine would indicate that there is only one other explanation."

Come to think of it, we don't have a problem with the concept of obeying at all, just as long as we get to play God. And let's face it: we're pretty sure we could do a better job.

In His absence, we have raised up a new "G" word: Gifts. We parents use it a lot to describe our extraordinary children. Athletic trainers and drama coaches and others who make their living off enriching the lives of short people have learned to toss the word around like confetti at parades in our young prodigies' honor. In reverent hushes they inform us, "your child has a gift," and we nod, "buttons bursting in the silence.

"Hermione has a gift," we share with our friends, humbly, incessantly. "They say she could go on to clog dance internationally."

Although we're usually overestimating the size and the scope and the magnitude of the ability, we're not wrong. Our children do have gifts. Us, too. Mine include, in no particular order, writing, teaching, leadership, administration, shepherding, and prophecy. When I consider these gifts, I thank God for them. When I say that my children, Graham and Remy, have gifts, I know where they came from and I know who knows best what they're for. I can't hear God's voice for my kids, but I can watch and listen and pray and adjust and try not to screw up whatever He has planned for their lives. And although I can't make them listen to God, or even want to, I can plant enough seeds to swing the world in their favor. That said, as I navigate my day surrounded by the parents of gifted children (notice there aren't any average kids anymore—only Gifted and Disposable), here's where I get confused: if a person believes in gifts but not in God, then where—as they stand in daily admiration of their child's emergent uniqueness, their heart swelling with pride and joy and, yes, gratitude — where, then, do they send the thank-you note?

Elijah's gift was prophecy. Today we think of that word as being synonymous with fortune telling but in the early days of the Judeo-Christian world it was the act of delivering God's word to His people. Sometimes it would be a vision for the future, but more often it was a warning of the consequences of straying from the right path. Prophets, in other words, were the world's first buzz busters, and no one knew how to break up a party like Elijah. In Elijah's day, the host of the "party" was King Ahab who **"did more to provoke the anger of the Lord, the God of Israel, than had all the kings of Israel before him,"** marrying Jezebel, a heathen foreigner, and indulging her passion for pagan gods. Baal was her favorite, a god made in metal shop in the shape of a bull, all snort and power and lust. High atop a hill, a location that Yahweh had forbidden for worship, Ahab built an altar for his nefarious bride's bull and began bowing down beside her, the masses falling like dominoes behind them. Jezebel smiled. She had converted the priests and the prophets. Those who couldn't be bought had been killed. The people—so easily swayed!—had quickly forgotten about things like trusting in God and relying on Him for all one's needs. Manna in the desert was old news and who would want to eat that stuff anyway?

Just outside their dark cloud, Elijah looked on. He watched as the people turned away from the LORD, as God's prophets were slaughtered, as mothers and fathers traded in the commandments for jollies. Until well into middle age, he pondered all this in his heart, turning the passages he'd been taught as a boy over again and again in his prayers. Everything he needed to understand about that moment in time seemed to have been spelled out by God through Moses in the book of Deuteronomy (11:8-17):

"Keep, then, this entire commandment ... so that you may live long in the land that the Lord swore to your ancestors ... a land flowing with milk and honey..."

The Land of Milk and Honey was intended to be a carefree and happy place, God's gift to his people after nearly 400 years of slavery in Egypt and the long, hard exodus that followed. But God's choice of the phrase "milk and honey" was, above all, a mnemonic device to help ensure their survival:

"...For the land you are about to occupy is not like the land of Egypt, from which you have come, where you sow your seed and irrigate by foot like a vegetable garden. But the land you are crossing over to occupy is a land of hills and valleys, watered by rain from the sky, a land that the LORD your God looks after..."

By the time the people of Israel had crossed the desert and settled into the Promised Land, all of God's good advice, as well as the terms & conditions, had become background noise.

"If you will only heed his every commandment … loving the LORD your God, and serving him with all your heart and with all your soul—then he will give the rain for your land in its season, the early rain and the later rain, and you will gather in your grain, your wine, and your oil: and he will give grass in your fields for your livestock, and you will eat your fill."

Every good thing was theirs for the taking, and take they did, quickly forgetting the giver of the Gift. This, too, God had foreseen, spelling out the risks and the consequences in advance: **"…Take care, or you will be seduced into turning away, serving other gods and worshipping them, for then the anger of the LORD will be kindled against you and he will shut up the heavens, so that there will be no rain and the land will yield no fruit, then you will perish quickly off the good land that the LORD is giving you."**

There were hundreds of thousands of people living in the region at that time, children and adults, the wise and the feeble, most of them descendants of Moses's covenant with God. But only one seemed to recognize that the instructions they had been given so many years before had been referring to such a time as this. Only one seemed to understand that he was to be both praying the drought into existence, and proclaiming that God's will had been done. Surely seeds had been planted in others as well; there may have been a thousand potential Elijahs. A thousand children made immortal by the simple act of loving and listening to the LORD their God. A thousand young Jewish boys or girls whose names could have gone on to be uttered breathlessly at Seders now catered by Whole Foods.

Or maybe the job was always meant for Elijah alone. That he alone was born for this purpose. That he alone did the very things he needed to do to become one of the greatest prophets ever known, and every day of his formative years—every lesson, every setback, every quirk of his preternatural mind—had been in some small way a preparation for the first public revelation of his Gift. We'll never know for sure. The truth of Elijah's life, as with each of our lives, lies somewhere between metrics and mystery.

What we do know is that midway through the reign of King Ahab, in the final years of the 8th century BCE, there was a terrible drought. And on the day the drought began, it was Elijah the Tishbite, of Tishbe in Gilead, who stepped through the crowd to approach the King, and with no fanfare or discussion, spoke 25 simple words—his first utterances in recorded history—that set the events of the next three and a half years in motion:

"As the Lord the God of Israel lives, before whom I stand, there shall be neither dew nor rain these years, except by my word." (1 Kings, 17:1)

Chapter 2

I'm not what you'd call a *Harry Potter* fanatic. It's not a religious issue for me—I read the first book and loved it; I just didn't feel a need to keep going. My husband Lon, on the other hand, was one of those who couldn't get enough, pre-ordering each new release. Graham stopped after three or four of them. His sister, Remy, listened to one or two. But Lon, he read them all and even bought the entire series on audiotape for family road trips, a fact that I shared with a Benedictine monk friend of mine at lunch one day.

"Really?" Father Luke said, betraying a boyish enthusiasm. "Could I borrow them?" This is a man who is an MD, an M.Div., an ordained priest, and an Oxford-educated Ph.D. He spends his days driving back and forth between a monastery and a seminary where he teaches mystical theology, medical ethics, the wisdom of the early Desert Fathers, and *lectio divina*, the ancient prayer practice of listening for God's word in daily scripture readings. "I could listen to them in the car while I'm driving," he said, an image which gave me as much delight as a Christmas stocking.

There are three things from *Harry Potter* I'll never forget. One was the little closet that Harry was forced to live in under the stairs, and how his seclusion and rejection and utter lack of extra-curricular anything could somehow only lead to greatness. The second was the train that whisked them all off to Hogwarts. I love any story with a train. I'm secretly hoping there's a plan to let me make my final exit on some celestial version of the Orient Express. For all my talk of the joys of solitude and prayer closets, I'm still a sucker for a man in uniform saying, "Will there be anything else, Madame?"

But the idea that I loved most profoundly from *Harry Potter* is the concept of the Sorting Hat. What could be cooler than a supernatural body of wisdom far greater than our own—a force that knows who we are and what we can do and which House we need to be in for all of that to unfold—and just like that, it speaks the Word aloud and our one, true life begins? The moment we hear it we know that any other House would have been folly because there can be no greater life for us than stepping moment to moment along our own wholly-customized path. I think we love the Sorting Hat because each one of us is, to varying degrees, afraid that we'll get it wrong, this thing; life. But most of all, I think we long for a Sorting Hat because despite all our bluster about charting our own course and seizing the day and being the masters of our own destiny, deep down we suspect that, much like our One True Love, there is actually such a thing as a Life we were Meant to Lead and wish from the bottom of our drifting souls that someone would tell us what it is.

No sooner had Elijah proclaimed boldly the coming drought than God told him what to do next: **"Go from here and turn eastward, and hide yourself by the Wadi Cherith, which is east of the Jordan. You shall drink from the wadi and I have commanded the ravens to feed you there."** (1 Kings 17:3)

In other words, get out of Dodge. Lay low. Do not waste your time looking for food or water. These will be provided, by ravens no less, leaving Elijah all day and all night to do—what? The first time I studied this story, Graham was a junior in high school, and all I could think about was all that time Elijah had on his hands. It was then I heard a voice as clear as my own, spoken with a Yiddish flair: *"Well as long as you're going to be down at the Wadi Cherith all day, you might as well take your SAT prep book with you, brush up on some of your Latin roots."*

It was the kind of thing I would have said, what many a doting mother ever vigilant in her quest to hoist her spawn into a bright future would have said. Even those of us who know the value of silence and prayer. Because the blitzkrieg that is the assessment of our children's worth as defined by a test designed by man has the capacity to bring fear and trembling to even the most faithful among us. In the past two decades, the business of preparing our children to look good on paper as they leave high school has grown into a $5 billion industry. A quick search on Amazon will reveal over 500 SAT preparation titles, all of which promise to give you and your child "that little edge"—those few extra points that will make the difference between a life of infinite worth and a legacy of missed opportunities.

Nothing could be further from the intent of the SAT creators. In the early 1940s, Harvard University President, James Bryant Conant, had grown increasingly concerned that America was turning into a truly undemocratic society. Years of watching his ivied halls fill with sons of alumni and grand-alumni with or without any particular spark of their own—had convinced him that he was playing a role in creating "a hereditary ruling class." His hope was to make Harvard a beacon of meritocracy and that all U.S. universities would become breeding grounds for a new elite "made up of brainy, elaborately trained, public-spirited people drawn from every section and every background." It was to be a distinctly American take on the French concept of *noblesse oblige* and the biblical mandate that **"from everyone to whom much has been given, much will be required"** (Luke 12:48). All Conant needed was a test that would help to determine who those truly gifted young people were.

Enter Henry Chauncey, psychometrics wonk, devout Episcopalian, and soon to be chief of the Educational Testing Service. After a time of prayer in the winter of 1945, he recorded this in his diary: *"... during Church this morning a thought occurred to me which though not new was amplified in its implications. There will undoubtedly in the near future be a greater emphasis on taking a census of our human resources in terms of capacities for different kinds of employment ... This project requires consideration from a lot of angles but men of vision in the field of testing, vocational guidance, government, economics, education could be consulted individually and eventually in groups..."*

What Chauncey had envisioned as a Sorting Hat for all Americans was ultimately trumped by Conant's belief that any effort to serve the common good must begin with identifying the best and the brightest. By the 1960s, the two intellectually gifted and spiritually magnanimous men had worked together towards differing visions to make the SAT the most widely accepted entrance exam at the most prestigious universities in the country, unwittingly blighting the landscape of higher education forever.

The test worked well enough, but it was quickly apparent that Conant had given our brightest young people too much credit: they were not, it turned out, particularly interested in using their gifts for the common good. In a single generation, the SAT had converted America's top universities into finishing schools for "well-paid, securely positioned providers of expert advice: corporate lawyers, investment bankers, management consultants, high-end specialized doctors." Not the study of ending poverty, or the creating of sustainable energy policies, or the educating of underprivileged youth, or even, God forbid, the upholding of faith—all ties to the churches that had built these grand institutions had been loosened to the point of disconnection—no, it was money their hearts longed for. Before long, the math was so simple even a drop-out could understand it: High SAT score equals Ivy League School; Ivy League School equals get rich quick and stay that way for generations. With that, the SAT-prep industry was born, pioneered by Stanley Kaplan, and promising to middle class kids with aspirational parents a shot at the Golden Ticket and upper class kids with perfectly ordinary abilities a way to hold on.

I'm not what we'd categorize as a "math/science" person. Much as I admire those who are, none of the joy or flow or ease that one experiences when she is in her right House comes to me through numbers. So you might find it curious that I got a much higher score in the Math than the Verbal on my SATs. This is doubly ironic since I'd gotten a D in Algebra 2. My mom called in a tutor for a few months, cleared up the problem; coach a rat through a maze enough times and he'll learn the right way to get to the cheese. But I would quickly forget every root and cube of it, not taking math (or science) in my senior year, or my first two years of college, dropping out without any math or science credits at all for a job as a full-time copywriter.

I suppose the verbal aptitude must have kicked in right after high school; either that or the thing that the test measures has nothing to do with knowing how to use words to communicate. Either way, when it came to measuring who I was or what I could do—what I should do—the scores were all wrong. Harry Potter had it right. In the world of *Harry Potter*, a divining quill records the name of magically-gifted children at birth. There is no admissions test for Hogwarts because "you are either magical or you are not." With the advent of the SAT test-prep industry, Hogwarts was officially open for business, the Sorting Hat was now for sale, and everyone—regardless of natural interests, ability, temperament, background, or intelligence—was being coached to gun for Slytherin, the House of "those cunning folk who use any means to achieve their ends." Net worth, baby, that's how you keep your options open. If we have nothing else to teach our children it's the importance of options. How else will we ensure they'll never end up like Elijah, reliant on the goodwill of ravens?

Trouble is, when we make our kids compete for a spot in a House that is not really theirs, we force them to resort to desperate measures. And so it should come as no surprise that across the globe, academic cheating is occurring at levels so consistently high and widespread that it is now the student who doesn't cheat that would be considered the aberration. This is not only true at the middle and high school level but also, and even more critically, at colleges and graduate schools, the training grounds for the next generation of leaders. Fittingly, the field of graduate study with the highest rate of cheating is business. MBA professors explain that many business classes are numbers based with one-right-answer kinds of tests, which are easier to cheat on than the essay-style exams often found in the arts and soft sciences. Maybe. They also suggest that people who are likely to sign on for an MBA program may simply be born with a "bottom-line mentality," so that engaging in what they view as a minor ethical lapse to ensure they get the MBA seal of approval is just a smart business decision—to them, an MBA is something bought, not earned.

A half century earlier, the men who graduated from Harvard Business School told a very different story. "They were not saints," says David Callahan, author of *Kindred Spirits: Harvard Business School's Extraordinary Class of 1949 and How they Transformed America*. These men of business were just as likely to tell a lie or rig a deal or stab a friend in the back. The difference was this: they did it for the sake of the business, not themselves. They were bottom-line thinkers, but the bottom line was not, to them, a personal slush fund. They took responsibility seriously. "They grew up during the Depression, fought in World War II, went to Harvard Business School on the G.I. Bill, and many came from the working class….They did not have a strong sense of entitlement. Wealth would be created patiently over many years."

Once America got a taste of overnight wealth, it became the only kind to aspire to. Where once men worked for the value of doing a good and useful thing, or the dream of building something grand and enduring, the 80s made too many too rich too fast and changed forever the face of our role models. We were suddenly a nation Entitled. Bigger cars, bigger homes, bigger closets. And if you couldn't afford the whole lifestyle, then at least you could get—with no money down and no payments till June— the big screen TV, drowning out any hope of hearing a different message.

As much as I'd love to hang around for a good wailing and gnashing over ethics and glut, there are more pressing, bottom-line concerns. As we speak, our shared prosperity is, in no small measure, reliant on the wisdom, acumen, and character of American business—the best efforts of the best and the brightest, but the "best and the brightest" seem to be either wholly self-interested or worse, utterly unprepared. They didn't do their homework. Their most creative problem solving was finding new and wilier ways to cheat. Up and down the halls of corporate America in this, the Great Recession, the question is being asked, "What do we do now?" And all around the tables, those who have faked their way into the job, whose only roadmap has been a Scantron, who never fully grasped the intricacies of finance or the nuances of market research, who overslept through the seminar on Doing Well by Doing Good, who bought their final paper on *Innovative Capitalism for the New Millennium* online, will have no choice but to rely on the skills that have gotten them where they are today. They'll bow their heads and check their smart phones and wait for an answer to fall from the sky, then take credit or assign blame accordingly.

When God led the Israelites out of slavery, they had some rough years. Forty of them, to be exact, spent walking across deserts that were too hot in the day and too cold at night. There was nothing to do to pass the time but question if they were really on the right road, and who put Moses in charge anyway, and really, wouldn't it just be easier to go back and be slaves. At least the menu was more varied. Six days a week they were blessed with morning dew and warm, nutrient-dense, fat-rich, honey-tinged flakes of manna raining down on them like a daily reminder of grace—and still they kvetched, tirelessly. They were not allowed to save the manna from one day to the next, warned by God through Moses that the insects would rot

27

the grain. One day at a time they were to wait for the manna, scoop it up and give thanks for it, shape it into little cakes and bake it on the hot stones. One day at a time they were to eat and live and continue their exodus till God delivered them to The Promised Land. One day at a time they were asked to trust and believe.

So God had the whole manna thing down. He could have just floated a nice funnel cloud of warm flakes over Elijah's personal campsite by the Wadi Cherith and called it a day. Instead He promised him food hand-delivered by ravens. The first time I ever read this story I thought, "Well of course, ravens are vultures and what better way to make a point about His sovereignty than to have a good, fresh nosh delivered twice-daily in the bills of obedient scavengers?" But ravens, I discovered, are more than just vultures. They eat carrion and maggots, to be sure, but also fruits, berries, nuts and grains, lizards, frogs, skinks, rats, mice, baby squirrels, spiders, ants and biblical, protein-rich locusts— basically, anything they can get their beaks on. **"The ravens brought him bread and meat in the morning, and bread and meat in the evening: and he drank from the wadi."** (1 Kings 17:6)

As the long punitive drought drew on, food of all kinds grew scarce. God needed helpers that had been gifted to handle lean times. He needed a way of building up Elijah's faith in His promise to provide each and every day. He needed a sociable creature—one that sparked to the sound of a human voice and enjoyed a good fireside caw— to keep Elijah from going mad with loneliness. God chose

His ravens to care for Elijah, and His ravens delivered. Right creatures, right spot.

As I neared the end of my 40s and recognized that there were limits on most of my earthly resources—time, money, brain cells—it was not always easy to trust in God's promise to provide. I wrote the $1300 dollar check each month to COBRA for our quickly-dwindling months of health care coverage and did battle with pangs and visions of myself at 70, toothless and rank with disease and standing outside the ER with a tin cup and a sign saying "But God told me to be a writer."

He had given me two promises to hold onto. One, a simple vision of me standing at a lectern, speaking once again before a crowd. I was no longer young. I could see myself slipping my reading glasses on as I began to share an excerpt from a new book. The reading glasses became for me a symbol of hope. While others bemoaned their loss of sight, I celebrated it. Each year I seemed to need more and more pairs, scattered about the house, until I realized one day that I probably spent more time with them on than off. Surely, my time was coming.

The second promise came in the form of a voice, a question, a proposition that I found to be more cruel than comforting: "What if you knew that you would write six books and none of them would be published, but then the seventh—the seventh—would become one of the great classics of modern literature? What would you do?" For a year, this was the voice that pressed in on my prayers and left me no choice but to carry on.

I've always made my living as a writer. My husband Lon would offer a slight correction: all the money I've ever made since I was 18 years old has been from writing. In the years I wrote screenplays and books that never sold, I would not have been able to live off the income. But manna comes in many forms, and live we did. Even when Lon's and my freelance advertising work came and went in fits and starts. Even when he built a small business and then saw it slowly destroyed before his eyes. Even when deals fell through and clients failed to pay and great work went unnoticed, there was always enough to get by on, enough to make sure that the kids had a nice life, that their real needs were met. We worried there wouldn't be. We made plans just in case. But something always came through, a morsel of nutmeat slipped in through the transom.

Midway through my 40s, it was safe to say that my fourth book, like the second and third ones before it, was not going to be sold. It was a good book, a worthy book— they all were—but deep down I knew, fiction was not my gift. I had turned to fiction after my first book—the first book I'd ever written— was published. *Baptism by Fire* was a wrenching memoir filled with intimate details about how I'd come to faith during a six-week window of time when Remy was diagnosed, at 8 months of age, with a brain tumor. My agent said I should write more books like that.

"More books about my daughter almost dying?!!"

"No, more books about mothers in crisis. You know, family stuff."

I knew I couldn't do that. I couldn't offer up my children's formative moments for copy. Anne Lamott does it beautifully. So does Amy-Julia Becker. But that was not my promised land. Or maybe I just didn't want it to be. Instead, I sent myself across a desert of fiction, where daily I honed the practice of praying and listening and writing, of showing up and believing and doing the work. It's a muscle like anything else. Page after page. Prayer after prayer. Gagging on manna. *God, please let someone publish this book.* Daily I wrote and the kids grew and the unsold manuscripts gathered dust.

What would I have done, I wondered, in Elijah's shoes, left alone by a drying creek with clear instructions to do absolutely nothing? There would likely be naps, lots of them. I would no doubt complain to the ravens about the lack of dipping sauces. I'm sure I'd make a little lean-to and find ways to decorate it, scratch a calendar in the dirt, turn a tumbleweed into a new best friend—all the things Tom Hanks did in *Castaway.* All the innovation and the solitude and the oneness and the madness and the obliviating despair, Elijah would have experienced all of it, except the one thing that kept me and Tom Hanks going. A goal. A purpose. We like to have a reason to get up in the morning. We need to have that reason, and this is why when God says hold up, wait, pray, it's not your time yet, our entire bodies rebel, legs kicking and flailing like some overturned dung beetle certain that if we try hard enough we might be able to gain a little traction on our own. God would have to admire the effort, wouldn't He?

But what if God *is* the goal? What if the entire purpose of our lives is simply to connect to Him? In *The Way of the Pilgrim*, a Russian peasant decides to spend his life walking the countryside, rubbing a prayer rope and reciting "The Jesus Prayer"—*Lord Jesus Christ, son of God, have mercy on me a sinner*—again and again and again, day and night, dark to light, until the words become his breath and pulse, and soon he finds that he is no longer aimless at all, but drawn in and to and through both perfectly ordinary and sometimes remarkable circumstances. He keeps a bag of bread crusts and a bodhi sac of water and he walks and he prays, sleeping in the woods or in the homes of benevolent strangers. He walks and he prays and he goes where God leads him and in doing so, he becomes rich in wisdom and peace, and his life, at long last, becomes his own.

Now that's just crazy talk. This is the Modern Era. We've evolved. We need sure things and the promise of more of them. We want to know where our next meal and our next mortgage payment and, if Suze Orman is right, our next six months of banked provision is coming from. We like our cushions and our back-up plans and if we have to tweak the contract with God to get it, well, ok then. Many would say "what contract?" but I believe that even if we've never been inside a synagogue or a mosque or a church— even if we have, and vowed never to go back—deep down in our striving hearts, beneath all the ambition and the fear, we suspect that we were made for a different sort of life. That when St. Augustine, the most dramatic convert of all time wrote that "our hearts are restless till they find their rest in You" it rang too true to ignore. If there really were such a thing as God, He would have to be our One True Love. And still we run. We run because we know what that means. He would want to move us out of our fat, happy ruts, or our sad, stalled days, and make changes on our behalf. He would want us to let Him be the Director of our Lives, and to teach our children to do the same. To trust Him even when it means long, slow periods of arduous, confounding drought. **"But after a while the wadi dried up, because there was no rain in the land."** (1 Kings, 17:7)

Lon had stood beside me patiently, believing in me, if not in God. He had given me what would seem like a lifetime to show that writing books was something I could make a living doing. I waited for God to confirm it with a second book contract, but it was not forthcoming. The wadi had finally dried up.

"I wish you could keep writing like this forever," Lon said, as close to tears as I'd ever see him. "But I can't do it alone anymore. I need to know we're in this together. I need you to go back to work full-time."

Like Dali's pocket watches the air between us melted. I found myself called back from the path where I'd been walking alone with my bag of bread crusts to the moment 22 years before when we had held each other's hands and taken our vows to work as one for life. "I'm sorry."

God moves in many ways, sometimes slowly, imperceptibly, so that one morning you wake up and realize

33

you're not the same person you used to be. Other times he moves more quickly—so quickly, if fact, that it may take years to recognize that in those long, hard desert times God had simply been setting the stage for the next source of provision: **"Then the word of the LORD came to him** (Elijah) **saying, 'Go now to Zarephath, which belongs to Sidon, and live there; for I have commanded a widow there to feed you.'"** (1 Kings 17:8-9)

A few weeks after we'd recommitted to a shared vision of how to move forward, Lon was offered a full-time job he didn't even apply for. For years, this creative advertising hot shop wouldn't even return his phone calls, and now, suddenly, there was a three-day freelance gig that turned into a rare and startling offer of a salaried position. On the exact same day, I was called in for an interview—first one I'd been on in years. Must have been my eager, heartfelt cover letter that did it: "Here's my resume and portfolio link. If you'd like to meet with me, I'm available." It was a new company, a tech darling start-up endeavoring to re-envision advertising for a new age. They needed a new Creative Director with traditional agency experience. I found myself actually feeling excited. After years of working alone, I would reenter the flow of people and ideas and the shared buzz of coffee and possibility. More than that, I would get a much-needed rest from the torments of fruitlessness. After 15 fiscally unpredictable years of working for ourselves—and with no more effort than showing up—Lon and I each rejoined the ranks of the fully employed in exciting new jobs that paid well, had full benefits and stock options, and showed great potential for interesting work.

Sometimes God just likes to show off.

Chapter 3

What were your favorite picture books growing up? Mine were *Where the Wild Things Are* and *The Giving Tree* and *Horton Hatches the Egg* and *The Smells of Christmas.* Graham loved *Goodnight Moon, Alexander and the Terrible, Horrible, No Good, Very Bad Day, Mike Mulligan and his Steam Shovel, The Battle of Sir Cob and Sir Filbert, Moe & Arlene in Tropical Paradise, Cloudy with a Chance of Meatballs, The Steadfast Tin Soldier* —the list goes on. Remy wasn't much into books but if she had to pick a few favorites they would have been *Harold and the Purple Crayon* and *Blueberries for Sal* and *Skateboard Monsters.* Disguised as nothing more than pure fun, picture books teach critical thinking skills, nurture imagination, and help kids develop an understanding of visual communication—an essential 21st century skill.

Tragically, in 2010, the sale of picture books was at an all-time low. Where even a decade ago, major publishing houses would fill up nearly half of their catalogues with picture books, many are now down to as little as 10%. When asked about the disappearing interest in this classic form, bookstore owners and publishers cite one reason above all others: parents are pushing their kids to start reading chapter books at a younger and younger age in the hopes of giving them that little edge, fearful that if they miss a month of precocious growth they will somehow be left behind.

We have convinced ourselves that only serious reading counts. I'm as guilty of this as anyone. Once the obvious picture book ages had passed I was eager for the kids to move on to chapter books and love them. Graham did, in fits and starts. Sometimes he'd read no more than the bare minimum, other times, when his interest was piqued, he'd dive headlong into a series. In fifth grade he fell in love with the *Wizard of Oz* books. I never knew there was more than one, but as it turns out there are 40 of them, 14 by L. Frank Baum and the others by writers who carried on his Oz legacy. Graham tracked down each one of them from libraries and bookstores all over the city, making it his own personal quest.

Remy, on the other hand, never read any of them—never even saw the movie. When a family commissioned her, at the age of 15, to paint a mural that celebrated their daughter's new found love for ice skating, Remy envisioned showing the girl in the costume she'd worn for her first competition season skating to the song "Somewhere Over the Rainbow." Paintbrush in hand, Remy was forced to phone a friend. "You know the girl, from Wizard of Oz?"

"Dorothy?" her friend replied.

"Yeah, I guess. What color hair does she have?"

The mural is quite wonderful. She had designed it all in Photoshop to scale with a deep background of Oz, and a middle ground showing Dorothy holding Toto overlooking a pool of blue-white ice and, in the foreground, the little girl spinning in her blue and white checked pinafore, skates covered in red. Remy had taught herself everything she knew about painting on a grand scale by practicing on her own walls—a mural every month or so, with occasional guidance from Lon—until she ran out of white space and felt ready to take her skills on the road.

In the summer before her junior year, she was assigned to read *The Red Badge of Courage* for Honors English. I cannot imagine many 16 year-old girls having any interest in that book, but she was diligent, introducing herself to online Spark Notes and filling out 10 pages of busy work without ever having gotten past page three of the actual novel. Despite her moral angst over this, she had finally figured out what most kids had realized long before, what I had spent a decade as a Junior Great Books leader fighting to change. The system isn't set up to care about actual reading. Just give 'em the answers they want to hear and you'll be golden.

I have no formal research to support this, but after many years spent alongside kids of every aptitude, from both private and public schools, I feel confident in claiming that the only students who are actually reading assigned books in high school anymore are the ones who get the same consuming joy from literary fiction that others get from crushes or robotics or hitting home runs. Formal research on the subject of children and reading was done recently by the University of Tennessee, and funded by the Department of Education. For three years the researchers invited low-income grade school kids to a spring Book Fair. One group of children was allowed to take any 12 books they wanted for free. The other group was allowed only activity books and games. The books the kids chose would make most educated parents cringe: *The Autobiographies of "The Rock"* and *Brittney Spears, Nascar's Greatest Drivers, Hannah Montana's Keeping Secrets,* and *Captain Underpants and the Big, Bad Battle of the Bionic Booger Boy.*

At the end of the three-year period, the kids who had spent the summer reading what most would consider sub-grade-level junk had bested the control group not only in reading, but across the board, an equivalent boost to having taken three years of summer school. I don't like it any more than you do—would much prefer to boast about my kids being really into Plato by puberty—but there it is. If we let kids follow their childish interests they will actually learn and grow and ignite all the requisite synapses no matter how much it mortifies us, their doting parents.

September 13th
It was the first day of Remy's junior year.
I dropped her off in front of
Venice High School,
drove home,
said my prayers,
and typed out in the center
of a new blank page,

"Elijah and the SAT."
The title had been on my heart
for three and a half years.
Now, it was time to begin.

Remy is a figure skater, a theatrical figure skater, to be exact. She proclaimed from out of the blue at the age of 11—I'll never forget the day; it was Good Friday— that this was to be her passion and she's skated almost every day since then. For the past five years, she'd put in two hours each morning before school and, in the evenings, taken dance and conditioning activities to support her development. Most days she's exhausted. In terms of academics, she's a highly conscientious student who freezes up when it comes to taking big tests. She's succeeded in high school thus far because she's figured out how to bolster her scores by doing every homework assignment, earning every extra credit point, and making her projects so thoughtful and creative that there would be no way to think of her as anything other than an A student.

But the SAT is the Mount Everest of big tests, and this was the year she would be expected to take it. If we cared about her future, we were supposed to make her take them more than once, make her keep taking them and practicing for them until she got something close to a respectable score. I could have pulled her off the ice, forced her into an aggressive schedule of SAT test-prep courses, tried to make her into something that looks more like the world wants a child to look on paper at 16. But I didn't. I had been a gymnast as a teenager. Never stood a chance at

Olympic gold but the striving gave me the self-discipline and the perseverance and the confidence I would need to become a writer. Every morning as we backed out of the driveway in the predawn hush, we said our prayers and trusted that it would all work out somehow.

I was not always this Zen about things. When Graham was in 7th grade—the year that counts if you plan to apply to private high schools—he decided to take a little break from being the well-behaved, good student he'd been for his entire grade school career. He started coming home boasting of the most demerits in the whole class, with report cards that looked like they'd been put in the wrong backpack. He seemed to be talking a lot in class. When I suggested to him that he asked to be moved away from whoever it was that was distracting him he said proudly, "Oh no, Mom, I like talking with almost everyone." Try as I did to get him to understand just how critical his seventh grade year was to any future options, he just kept laughing and playing and looking unconcerned about having Cs where the As and Bs used to be. He was 12. Obviously, outside help would be needed. I signed him up for an ISEE prep course in Brentwood, given by a man I had known as a child, a lifelong educator, a new role model for Graham I had hoped.

In the opening chat with the parents, the test-prep guru asked what I assumed was a rhetorical question. "What are you really looking for when it comes to choosing a high school for your child?" The parents all smiled knowingly. I thought to myself, "A place that's a good fit for his talents. A place where he can grow into himself. A place— "

My thoughts were interrupted by what I would soon discover was the right answer. "Picking a high school is about picking your child's social group. Pick the right friends now and it'll pay off for years to come." I went wall-eyed and panned the room; all the lovely, tan, and older parents nodded knowingly. Had I heard it correctly? Had a professional educator just said that choosing a high school was all about social networking? I went to chat with him after class, maybe make a little joke about his comment.

"I was surprised when I looked over your son's preliminary practice test," he said. "Would have expected a little more horsepower from a child of yours."

How dare you, I thought, but smiled weakly. "Well, that's why he's here."

For eight weeks, I drove Graham to a meeting room in the upscale Brentwood neighborhood where I had grown up. There he was surrounded by kids who'd had assessment-test readiness built into their academic days since circle time—they could fill in bubbles in their sleep. Graham took the ISEE, the requisite admissions exam for most secular private schools in America, and got a perfectly average score. He was accepted into the only private school we applied to primarily on the basis of his athletic ability. He had never wanted to go to a private high school, had only jumped through the hoops because I had insisted it was important to see what his options were.

"Mom, I just want to go to Venice High," he told me. "I don't want to go to a school with a bunch of privileged white kids. I'm sure it's a good school. But I think I'll learn a lot more about the world at Venice, so even if it's

43

not quite as good in terms of classes and everything, I think it'll be better in the long run." That's how he said it. Clear as day. At 13.

So off he went to Venice High School, and, even though I suspected it had a lot to do with him wanting to play baseball for the coach there, I knew he had made the right choice. He was put on the varsity baseball team as a 13-year old freshman and spent his days on the field with 18-year olds who struggled to be eligible, to stay out of trouble, to graduate at all. He was a pitcher and an outfielder and played year-round ball not only in high school but in the most competitive scout leagues in Southern California. At 14 he represented the city of Los Angeles in an international tournament sponsored by Major League Baseball; they had bodyguards and everything. He played practice games at Dodger Stadium and Comerica Park. He pitched against the country of Puerto Rico. Everyone thought he had what it took to play at a top DI college, but by the time his senior year rolled around, his lean frame would be 20 pounds, and his fastball 5 mph, shy of the mark.

There had been 1200 students in Graham's freshman class. Come graduation, there were only 350. A hundred planned to go to college. Thirty of them at 4-year colleges, including Graham, who had a 3.3 GPA and well above average, but by no means Ivy League, SAT scores. The mound had been his classroom. He had figured out how to be successful by giving his heart on a field of grass with kids who grew up in the projects and others who would go on to The Show. He carries their stories with him, in him, everywhere he goes. He carries the tools of early morning wake-up calls, of long drives to faraway tournaments, of sitting in the dug-out, studying every play, of striking out the side, of not being able to get out of the inning, of letting grades slip and then digging out of a hole on time, of passing up parties and shortcuts and distractions. He carries the memory of the former player killed by gang fire, of building a garden in his honor, of Lon carefully weeding it during practices. He could tell you the batting averages of every player in the league that'd ever donned a uniform, and the kink in their character that would make them fail. He had learned to lead, and he had learned to follow. And with all eyes upon him, he knew how to stand alone, shut out the noise, and get the job done, a skill that can only be measured in the real world.

"[Elijah] **set out and went to Zarephath. When he came to the gate of the town, a widow was there gathering sticks; he called to her and said, 'Bring me a little water in a vessel, so that I may drink.'"** (1 Kings: 17:9-10)

I'm sure there were a lot of widows living in the seaside town of Zarephath at that time. It was a town along a public road that hugged the shore of the Sea of Galilee, all that salt water driving the drought-stricken Galileans mad. A sip of water was not a small request. Only the right widow—his widow—would have granted it. These divinely appointed people rarely wear nametags. Those of us who attempt to recognize the people, the moments, that are put in our path to somehow make all of our lives better, have learned to use the old Richard Scarry technique: Stop, look, and listen.

I had a meeting at church at noon with our new Vicar, an apprenticing pastor who we hoped would stay on with us when his time was through. We were making plans for a new Bible study on becoming Peacemakers. I needed to stop writing and didn't like where I was leaving off; I preferred to break with a fragment of what I'd pick up on when I returned. I wrote in this space, where the words are that you're reading right now, "need anecdote about how God choreographs our movement for His purposes and ours if we let him," and headed off to church.

It was a good meeting, short and productive. I needed to make some copies of poems for the Vicar, a task that involved source books in various page and font sizes, requiring tedious enlarging and cropping. A teacher from our day school came in and preempted me. I waited. I sighed. It was well past lunchtime and I was getting hungry to the point of moody. I made my copies and ran out through the kitchen.

The stretch of sidewalk between the church's back door and my car was no more than 15 feet. There, on the narrow patch of adjoining lawn, was the biggest, triple dollop of dog poop in the history of dung. Now, I am not a dog person but it occurred to me someone should pick it up. I continued towards the car, my lesser and greater angels beginning to arm wrestle over the outcome.

I'm not on the maintenance crew/ Yes, but you're the one who saw it. And it's your church just as much as anyone else's/ But

I'm starving, and it'll be easier to pick up later when it's dry/ But you're the one who saw it and you're the one who thought that someone should pick it up. I dropped all my books and papers in the car and turned back around. When God gives you a book to write you don't take any chances.

In the kitchen, there was a stack of paper towels; the stiff, folded kind we filled the bathroom dispensers with. I scooped the vile blob up, holding it out in front of me like cymbals in a climactic percussive passage until I realized— Oh crap!—I couldn't just throw it out in the kitchen trash. I headed out through the parish hall, into the breezeway that led from the church to the school where the kids were finishing up their midday recess. I was not peaceful. I was not a cheery helper. I wanted someone to notice so I could get some credit for it. If anyone asked what I was doing I planned to say, "I'm storing up treasure in heaven" and hoped they'd be impressed both by my generous heart and my scholarly knowledge of scripture. But no one asked.

As I crossed through the narrow breezeway to the dumpster, I saw the kindergartners lining up. There was a young boy off to the side hugging an older boy with all his might, blocking his path, trying his patience. I emptied my hands. As it happened, I knew the little boy who hugged with such ferocity. Two weeks into the new school year, I was probably one of the few people who did.

"Hey Lucas," I shouted, as the day care helper tried to gently coax his arms free. "I could sure use a hug like that. You think I could have one?"

He was a young friend from the neighborhood. He'd had a rough start in life and was now getting his first

47

taste of a stable, loving community. He had an enormous heart. At the sound of my voice, he looked up, let go of the older boy, and ran towards me like a linebacker. Lucas is built like a St. Bernard. I braced myself as he leapt at me, stomped his oversized sneaker on my sandalled foot and threw his arms around me so hard that my sunglasses flew off my head and I found myself regretting instantly that I hadn't done more Kegels. I hugged him back and kissed his head as my toe throbbed and I could see on the ground that a lens had popped clear out of my frames.

"What are you doing here?" he said all floppy arms and sweaty cheeks and puppy dog smile. His need for belonging was like some giant sucking thing. You could feel his whole body drawing it right out of you.

"I just came to give you a hug," I said.

Lucas beamed, then dashed off to take his place in the row of kindergartners ready to return to their room for a picture book and some much needed quiet time. The day care teacher smiled thanks as I walked back through the parish hall. My toe pulsed as I struggled to squeeze the lens back into the frames with my dog-cootied hands. It was not how we expect to feel when we are in the middle of a divinely choreographed moment. It was messy and it hurt a little. I got back in the car and burst out laughing. Here I was thinking I was doing God a great big favor cleaning up His yard and tending to His sheep and all along he was just trying to give me the next page of this book.

Chapter 4

Lon doesn't really believe that God is real or living or communicative, but when he was a junior in high school he had a voice shouting inside of him so loudly it drove him to override every influence of his military family.

"I want to study art in college," he said.

His parents, with no reason to believe that this was a practical thing to do, said, "Ok."

Virginia Commonwealth University was so unimpressed with his abilities that they made him take remedial art the summer before his freshman year. He did, and his skills grew. He developed a keen sense of commercial messaging and design. Got his first job right out of school at a little four-man shop in Virginia Beach. A few years later he realized, not vaguely but urgently, that if he didn't get out of there he'd never amount to anything. He flew to California, interviewed at a big-time agency, got hired on the spot, and moved to L.A., where we met at work a few months later.

A lot of folks will call these psychic nudges intuition, as if the knowledge originates from some prescient inner-guide—supernatural, maybe, but certainly not God. Intuition is a powerful thing and we do tend to know ourselves better than anyone else and if we don't believe in God well, then, it's unlikely that we'll credit Him with any good advice. When everything works out perfectly, what could be more satisfying, after all, than patting our own intuition on the back? But the flip side is the true litmus test. If you're on any sort of truth-finding journey, try this: next time a disbelieving friend finds out that a loved one has fallen seriously ill, or their spouse has been laid off, or their house stands burning in flames and they fall to their knees and begin to wail, lean in, listen closely. See if it's Intuition they cry out to to save them.

"Now 'Bring me a morsel of bread in your hand,' Elijah said. But the widow said, 'As the LORD your God lives, I have nothing baked, only a handful of meal in a jar, and a little oil in a jug; I am now gathering a couple of sticks, so that I may go home and prepare it for myself and my son, that we may eat it and die.'" (1 Kings 1: 11-12)

It always comes down to provision. Elijah needs some. The widow is running out. Life hangs in the balance for all of them. There is clearly not enough food. Anyone can see that. How many times have we looked at our checkbooks and thought we're not going to make it. We'll survive this month, maybe the next one. But then it's over. The wadi will be dust. Wealthy people suffer the same base fear. Soon they'll be exposed, their fortunes reversed, just like all the sensible little people who'd stored up their grain, confident they had provision for life, and then in the blink of a fiscal quarter, were robbed blind. How can God be so cruel? I can't speak for Him, but I do know it's a lot easier to see grace when the cupboards are bare.

Lon and I had started back to the corporate advertising world one week apart. Eighteen months later, again, one week apart, we were each laid off—him, then me. It was the biggest quarter of job losses in the U.S. in a decade. What little bit of freelance work there was would now be vied for by thousands of talented, unemployed, creative people. We began to look at the prospects of our life for the coming year: at the cost of keeping the house, of letting Remy stay with her skating, of covering Graham's car insurance, of college, health care, retirement, old age. In eight months Lon would be 55; if we could only hold onto the house till then, we could sell it, invest the money, live off it if we had to. Maybe it was time for a change. We looked at job listings all over the country, envisioned fresh starts. "We could get a little townhouse in Portland," I'd say and we tried to imagine it. I'd check out the local high schools, the ice rinks, the online homeschooling options just in case the fresh start was temporary.

God had tried to warn me. A week before I was let go, I was on a red-eye home from New York, when I was suddenly seized with a message so intrusive I bolted upright from a dazed sleep nearly toppling my 7&7 and a half-eaten bag of Jelly Bellies. *Call University of Phoenix. Finish your degree.* Well that didn't sound right. I still had a job. I mean, I knew there would be lay-offs, but I was certain it wouldn't be me. Nothing would make less sense than it being me.

I hadn't thought about the University of Phoenix for a long time. Technically, I was already enrolled, had even studied independently and taken two CLEP exams to cover the 6 required science units. But instead of becoming a full-time student, I had become a full-time boss, and the demands of my new position made even the online program impossible. Besides, I had no real use for a bachelor's degree. All I knew was that I couldn't enroll in a master's program without one.

I was laid off in a herd. One hundred and twenty-five people led into a room where we were dismissed en masse while the IT folks stripped our laptops bare. It was the day before the presidential election. Somewhere in between the warning on the plane and the uncertainty of the days that had led us to this holding cell, I made a vow: if—when—I finally went back to get my degree out of the way, I'd tackle the math first. The math had been the thing that had kept me from considering a degree path, even as I took dozens of college classes for the sheer love of learning. If I had to take math I would do it my own way, in my own time, at my own pace. On November 4th, 2008, I woke up and voted for a new future. Then I came home, rifled through the kids' bookshelves, found an old copy of *Painless Algebra*, opened the first page and began.

"'Do not be afraid,' Elijah said to the widow. 'Go and do as you have said; but first make me a little

cake of it and bring it to me, and afterwards make something for yourself and your son.'" (1 Kings 17:13)

God knows how we get. We're fearful of every little thing. It's no surprise that the most common greeting used by angels and prophets is, "Do not be afraid." God knows when He shows up to give us our marching orders we tend to go weak in the knees. Notice Elijah's request. He does not ask the widow if she has any scraps or crusts or crumbs. God doesn't want our scraps. He's not interested in us leading lives where we do every single thing we can think of first and then, if there's any time leftover, we might, if we remember, say "oh, by the way, thanks." He wants our first fruits, our first breath, the first things first from our primary gifts—you know, the ones He gave us. In exchange, He'll give us everything we were ever meant to be or do in a shape and form and sequence and flow ultimately far richer and more rewarding than anything we could come up with on our own, providing for our every real need, and making the world a little more like Heaven on earth while He's at it.

Most of us don't even have a file in our brains in which to put a thought like that anymore. We've been trained to worship good job prospects above all else by a shop-and-spend economy that feeds off steady incomes and a he-who-dies-with-the-most-toys culture that keeps us laughing through our tears. But sooner or later, suppressed souls rebel, bubbling up in middle age in the form of depression or rage or disillusionment. By then it's too late to reclaim the whole of the life God wanted for us, but we can always fall on our crippling knees and beg for scraps.

"For thus says the LORD the God of Israel; the jar of meal will not be emptied and the jug of oil will not fail until the day that the LORD sends rain on the earth. She went and did as Elijah said, so that she as well as he and her household ate for many days. The jar of meal was not emptied, neither did the jug of oil fail, according to the word of the LORD that he spoke by Elijah." (1 Kings: 17:14-16).

Even if you've never read a word of the Bible, you probably could name at least one biblical example of provision lasting much longer or stretching much further than it should have. Think about it. Go ahead, I'll wait. You might have thought of the story of the loaves and the fishes (there are several of them actually), different times when Christ took a little bread and fish and turned it into enough to feed the Staples Center and send everyone home with a doggy bag. Or the time God made a day's worth of lamp oil last longer than humanly possible, which is remembered each year for nine days of Hanukkah. And if you're fond of a good wedding reception, you might have recalled Jesus' first miracle, where he turned water into an endless stream of the "finest wine," amazing and delighting the guests and kicking off, at his mother's urging, the beginning of the end. The point is this: God knows how to make stuff last. But who can really afford to believe it? Let's just say, for the sake of argument, that we give up our earthly to-do lists and start asking how He—whoever he is exactly— thinks we should spend our days and we even learn to pray and we even start to hear Him and then suddenly the worst happens: we run out of money. Or food. Or time. And we've got no back up plan. No cushion. Not even a well-connected friend to pull us back up when we fall.

It is this fear that drives us to drive our kids to aim for the big numbers, the sort of SAT scores that'll ensure they'll never run out of anything—ever. This is our legacy to them: we made sure they jumped so high that the world could never fail to pay them enough to make them feel safe and secure all the rest of their days. But for all the mathematical certainty of that equation, we don't feel sure at all.

It was February of her freshman year. Remy had been working on a new spin, a reverse camel spin, in which she enters quickly and forcefully on an inside edge. She had been so excited about it she even asked me to stand at the rail to watch. I crossed my arms against the chill as she picked up speed for her approach and— It happened so fast, the thud echoing through the rink, causing two former Olympians to look over and gasp. Her edge gave out from under her and she flew up and out and back, smack on the base of her skull. We waited for her to get up. I felt blurry inside as I watched her rise. But rise she did. Two days later, Natasha Richardson hit her head in much the same way on the slopes and never came home.

In addition to having had brain surgery as an infant, Remy had had one other hard blow to the head in her lifetime. Her class had been rehearsing for the major rite of passage at our little K-8 school: the 4th grade play. They were doing a vampy musical version of Cinderella with lip-synced tunes from Abba. Remy was cast as the wicked stepmother, a role that she adored. This was the year she first declared that she wanted to be an actress. Every day the director, a school parent who was a successful film and TV star, would tell me she had something special. Teachers who'd snuck a peek at rehearsals said she was at a whole other level. I couldn't say either way; Remy never wanted me to watch her in her preparations—not for theatre or skating or art. She liked to work on top-secret projects that she then revealed to me, watching closely for the level of delight and pride in my eyes.

On the day of her 4th grade fall, I had been at the school for Wednesday morning chapel with the kids and had just returned home, poured a cup of coffee, sat down to write. I was just thinking that maybe this would be the year she found her way to shine, when the phone rang.

"Heather, Remy's fainted," the principal said. "She hit her head pretty hard. She's sitting up now and conscious. They had just started their play rehearsal. I called an ambulance to have her checked."

When I got there, she was sitting in a huge wooden clergy seat near the altar, surrounded by paramedics. The play was held in the church, which was covered in Spanish tile. She had been standing upright, evidently delivering a line with so much cackle it took the breath right out of her: she suddenly fell straight back, no bend, no slouch, no buffer, flat on the back of her head.

"Don't take me to the hospital," she cried. "They'll cut my head open!!" It was the first time I realized how much she carried the memory of her surgery with her.

At the ER, they took some tests to clear her of anything serious. They watched her for a few hours, informing us that girls this age faint sometimes for no apparent reason. It had happened to me. Once. Just about the same age.

The fall on the ice resulted in a mild concussion. Remy took two weeks off before beginning work on her new dramatic program for the season. It was to be the year she finally got to skate to *Carmina Burana*, the haunting, angels vs. demons chant music she'd been begging to use since her first recital. The coaches had said it was a little "big" for a new skater. Now it wasn't. Remy generated the sort of power and drama on the ice that made her seem far more advanced than her jumping level. Day by day, her strength returned. The music inspired her. The program was starting to take shape. A new dress was ordered. Before we knew it, the spring recital was only a few days away. We packed up her skates, loaded her bag in the trunk, and, under the light of a new day, pulled onto the boulevard that led to Venice High School.

It seemed like a normal enough morning. The sun was shining. The radio was playing more commercials than music. The green lights were all going my way. I proceeded to cross the intersection—no reason not to, except for the fact that a mom on a cell phone ran the red light on the cross street, heading straight for my passenger side. I slammed on the brakes, heard the deadly shriek of tires, the heavy air of impending—what? The woman suddenly realized what she had done. I could see her teenaged son screaming at her as she gripped the wheel and bore down.

Smoke rose from her tires as she brought her van to a dead stop directly in front of me. I prepared to crash.

Two inches. That's how much space there was between my front bumper and the side of her car. One second. That's the margin of error that could have made that intersection into a crucible. One mph. Faster, slower, the calibrations would have been off and Remy would likely have been killed. The woman looked at me through her van window, down into my little sedan and quickly peeled away.

"Rem, are you ok?" Her seatbelt had held her firmly in place, her body untouched.

"I don't feel right," she said. "I feel weird."

The shock wore off by midday. Somehow she survived the week. The doctor gave her the ok to perform. It would have been hard to stop her. "You know me, mom. I could be in a wheelchair, but when it's time to put my glitter on, I'm good to go." She performed on a Friday night before a local crowd of friends and fans. It was a coming out, of sorts, a young skater declaring herself as a mature performer. She was winded, but thrilled.

On Monday morning, two days later, she had her first panic attack. She was studying anatomy at school and they were required to learn all the names of an entire structure each day; the strange words taunted her, refused to stick. There were daily tests. Daily pressure. The ice was the only place that gave her joy, but every time she got her heart rate up, the crush of the week would overcome her. The gargoyled voices of *Carmina Burana* shouted out through the loudspeakers each morning, setting the tone for the day. I wondered if the music was too much, if it was fueling the turmoil. Lon and I talked about making her change the program.

"No. This is my music. This is my time to skate it," she said, as if she knew something we didn't.

This was not my first experience with panic attacks. When Graham was in 10th grade he had been with a group of high-achieving classmates, studying for an AP World History test. No sooner had I dropped him off, I got a call to pick him back up again. I teased him about not taking the study group seriously enough, getting booted.

"Just hurry up," he said.

When I got there, four girls were hovered over one of their friends who was breathing into a paper bag and crying. They were stroking her legs and waiting for the ambulance to arrive. There were no adults in the house. I knew all of the girls. Had worked with most of them in an honor's book club I had volunteered to lead at Venice High.

"This is why 15-year olds should not be taking college classes," I shouted at Graham and his baseball buddy in the car on the way home. The image of that panic attack stayed with me as the symbol of how we have pushed our kids too hard, too fast, but now my own 15-year old daughter was having them, my daughter who was not in AP classes, who did not aspire to go to Harvard, or become a National Merit Scholar. She was an artist, through and through. Still, the symptoms belonged to the same disease: whatever it was they were trying to do, it was more than their vulnerable, young, high-achieving, dream-craving bodies could take.

The end of Remy's sophomore year was only two months away. We took it one day at a time. Skating. Homework. Life. Prayer. Days passed. Weeks. We were never certain how she would feel or how she would get through the day. Sometimes provision comes in the form of deep breaths and the passage of time. On rare occasions, it comes via teachers who allow good, conscientious students with As to skip the final exam.

Summer came. Remy was never overwhelmed in the summer. She trained and painted and babysat; she walked dogs for travelling neighbors and caught spiders to feed to her lizards and cut music for enough future skating programs to take her into old age. In August, Remy travelled to the World Arena in Colorado Springs to compete for the first time with 250 of the best artistic skaters—athletes of different levels and styles who had qualified in events all over the country—in the USFSA National Showcase for Theatrical Skating. I worried about the altitude. I worried about the pressure. I worried about everything, including the fact that an MRI taken as a precaution after her fall and her subsequent panic attacks had revealed a new cyst in her brain. Lon and I had decided not to tell her or anyone till after the competition. I made an appointment for her with the neurosurgeon the day after we were scheduled to return from Colorado.

As she took to the ice in the spotlight, the announcer read the introduction that she had written: "To me this music is the ultimate battle between life and death. And in the end, Life always wins."

Remy performed to the music of *Carmina Burana* just the way she'd been picturing it all those years, and walked away with the title: U.S. Teen Dramatic Champion. That night in our hotel room, I called my friends to joke and boast. "Well, it's official. I am now the proud parent of the most dramatic teenaged girl in America." But deep down I could not help but wonder to the point of trembling if God had given her that performance as a swan song.

On the plane back home I told her about the MRI. She nodded. When it came to real-life drama, Remy was eerily stoic. The neurosurgeon, Dr. Lazareff, had been apprenticing under Remy's surgeon when she was an infant; now he was a global superstar in Pediatric Neurosurgery, a wing in which I never thought we'd find ourselves again.

"Good morning, good morning," he said, his thick accent wafting like the scent of warm paella. He introduced us to the circle of residents who followed him around wherever he went. We nodded numbly and handed over the film, which he studied carefully before speaking.

"This is what we call an arachnoid cyst, yes. Not big. Not dangerous. It's like a little blister ball of fluid. Athletes get them a lot from falls. Just saw a boy across the hall, soccer player, big future. Has one twice as big. Not to worry."

"So we just leave it in there?"

"She's a figure skater, you said?" Remy and I nodded. "And she just went to a national competition, yes?"

"She won her whole division," I said foolishly.

"Then I think it's safe to say it's not causing her any neurological harm."

Remy grew pale. A single uncharacteristic tear streamed down her cheek, as if the magnitude of all that had been and all that could have been—still somehow might be—were hitting her just in this instant. The doctor rolled his stool closer to her, looked her right in the eye, "You're not going to die from this, ok. You're not going to lose any skills, or memory. Or hair," he said with a wink. "You're going to go on to have a wonderful life and you're going to invite me to your wedding, ok?" He patted her on the knee and rose to leave. "You're a national champion, got it?"

A glimmer of confidence returned to her pinking cheeks as Remy nodded, "True that." It was only then that I could fully enjoy the small miracle of that accomplishment.

Chapter 5

I passed my 6-unit CLEP test for College Mathematics the week before we went to Colorado. Nine months of taking myself from Pre-Algebra up through College Statistics, all online, all for free, all on my own. All while juggling a part-time freelance clientele that required me to travel all over the U.S. and Canada and a full-time online course load to complete the requirements for a B.S. in Management. My original plan had been a B.A. in Communications—figured I could phone it in—but a guardian angel in the counseling office had prevented me. "Oh good heavens, Heather, I can't let you sign up for something you could easily be teaching. The management classes will at least stretch you a little, give you some new tools the next time you're in charge of something."

Online colleges have a long way to go towards establishing widespread credibility, but I can tell you firsthand that the coursework is plenty rigorous. If you're the sort of person who takes things seriously, you can learn a great deal not only about the subject matter but about technology, virtual teamwork, and your own strengths and weaknesses. I didn't love my management classes, but I was good at them. I had to consider whether God might actually be calling me not to a new life of study and reflection but back to the advertising world to impact lives in a more big-picture way, maybe from a corporate ethics perspective. I could go on and do an MBA, secure something stable, give Lon a much-needed break from carrying so much of the load. I could. I would be good at it. Except for one thing. One essential element that would prevent me from ever being really excellent or moderately happy in business: I don't love money or titles or stuff. Sure, I enjoy many of the experiences that money can buy—a nice trip, an opportunity for my children, a massage—but I have never awakened a single day in my life and thought, "oh, to be rich."

But rich I was. Each day since the lay-offs I stood arms outstretched and watched in rapt awe as we were pelted with so much good work that we were able to pay all our bills, keep the house, let Remy keep skating, support Graham through college, pay off my own new degree, and, just because God likes to be perfectly clear about what He's really capable of, simultaneously erase a considerable debt we'd incurred on a credit line in the long, lean years preceding—debt we were somehow unable to make a dent in when we both had jobs. We were no longer slaves. We'd been carried out of the land of Egypt and fed heartily en route by the grace of God. I now stood at the ready, listening, eager for my next instruction.

September 22nd
Remy got off the ice early.

Ten days into her junior year,
the panic attacks had returned.
I prayed in silence as I drove her to school.
God slowed my spirit
to a near monotone chant.
It was the sort of steadying shift
I had come to recognize
as preparation for change.

I spent the morning building on earlier research about Elijah's life, adding subjects that included the terrain of the Exodus, the nature of vocation, the role of prophecy, the principles of human ability, the history of the SATs, and a range of benchmark thinking on aptitude and intelligence. I filled my Amazon cart with used books on a dozen subjects that to me felt very much related.

The first book arrived the next day. It was the one book that, in my mind, had the least to do with the essential research needed for *Elijah & the SAT*. "Skip the SAT, save thousands in tuition," the subhead boasted. It was not destined to become a classic, but its snack-sized pages served to awaken in me the spark of an alternative path: a rarely publicized test—the California High School Proficiency Exam—that allows 16 & 17-year olds, too young for the GED, to earn the legal equivalent of a high school diploma. It was considerably harder than the High School Exit Exam, but not as demanding as the SAT. Once passed, it allowed a student to begin community college full-time or to chip away at G.E. credits close to home, then transfer to a four-year college where there would be no review of high school transcripts or SAT scores. According to the website, the test was only given three times a year. The next one was in 24 days.

I went to church and filled out a prayer request asking for wisdom about major life decisions for Remy. I checked the box marked Confidential: <u>not</u> to be read aloud in church, but there was an oversight, and the prayer was read before the whole congregation. Evidently, she was going to need all the help she could get. On the way home, I found myself at Barnes & Noble, picking out a test prep book for the CHSPE, the first test prep book I ever bought without resenting it. I had only mentioned the possibility of this new option to Remy the day before. I wasn't entirely sure it wouldn't add more stress than it would relieve, but ever since the words came out of my mouth she looked like she could breathe again. When she saw the prep book in my hand, she literally leapt out of bed.

"We can wait till tomorrow," I said gently.

Remy likes to honor the Sabbath. She stays up late on Saturday nights to get her homework out of the way, doesn't allow herself to use her computer or do any exercise on Sundays. When she talks to God, it's usually from her bed.

"No," she said zealously. "Let's do this thing!"

For the next 3 ½ hours, she lay on the floor with a practice test and a calculator. Periodically, I would check on her progress, reporting to Lon that she seemed perfectly calm and utterly focused. He had always been an advocate of kids having normal, awful high school experiences, but

66

even he had begun to realize that something had to give. That night, I reviewed her essay and the answer sheets for English and grammar, reading comprehension, and math—the core components of the exam. If it had been a real test, she would have passed.

"Yeah," Lon said. "But that's in her own house, in her own room, with no strange faces or noises or ticking clocks. Not having to see everyone else finish early and start leaving while you're still working at it. That's what makes people anxious. That's going to be the test."

September 27th

It was projected to be the hottest day
on record in L.A. history—
113 degrees downtown.
Remy's morning skate had gone well.
Her drop-off at school was uneventful.

It was already warm. The neighborhood kids were playing in the street before they went off to preschool. I chatted with the neighbors in our cul-de-sac, just as I had all summer long. Over the past 14 years, we had developed the sorts of relationships that feel like the best of family and friends combined. Some have come and gone. My next-door neighbor Rachel has been there as long as we have. Her daughter, Freja, now goes to the same school where Graham and Remy went. Her son, Henry, is four. I have spent time with him every single day since he was born.

When he was baby, I would bring him in my room and let him play with my prayer pear, an earthen ceramic pear-shaped rattle that, according to the gift tag, alerted the angels to rising petitions. My friend Kate Campbell had picked it up for me at a monastery in Mississippi.

At 8:30 in the morning, it was already pushing 90 degrees. Henry and I sat on the stoop. I had a cup of coffee and Henry had a green apple Popsicle and we talked about his plans for the day.

"Is he good with you for a few minutes?" Rachel asked, a formality as she backed out of the driveway to take Freja to school.

I nodded and Henry and I smiled and waved, fluorescent green juice dripping down his chin as they drove off.

"Can I use the hula hoop?" Henry asked. It was a big heavy circus style one I kept inside; to a four-year old boy, it was much cooler than a prayer pear.

"What's the rule?" I said.

"Bring it back when I'm done," he smiled and he darted into the house. A few minutes later, his babysitter arrived and our time was up.

It was a productive day. I wrote for a few hours, documenting the events that had begun to take shape since the arrival of the first new research books. On a desktop Stickie I made a note as to where I'd left off on the Elijah narrative—specifically, the place in the passage at the widow's house where I was to pick back up the next day:

"After this the son of the woman, the mistress of the house, became ill: his illness was so severe that there was no breath left in him." (1 Kings: 17:17)

In the afternoon, I read more about the CHSPE guidelines, filled out the official form, sat in the bank to get the money order, and waited in line at FedEx to overnight it, wondering all the while why it was I needed the OK of someone in Sacramento to decide what was best for my child. Remy and I pulled in the driveway just as Rachel was packing up to take the kids to her mom's for a swim. Lindsay, the woman Rachel had fallen in love with two years before, was with her. We talked about the heat. After the coldest summer on record, where all we did was beg for sun, now everyone was cursing the warmth. How we honestly believe we've transcended our kvetching ancestors is beyond me.

"I love this weather," I said.

I felt happy in the thick heat in a way that was unlike any other happiness; it was visceral and spiritual at the same time. The air was the exact temperature of my skin, my body, my blood. I felt as if there was no difference between me and the realm of the unseen, as if I could simply dissolve into air, into spirit. It was not hard for me to imagine being lifted straight up to heaven, flesh turned to heat, rising. I tried to explain this to Rachel and Lindsay in words that would not seem too out there.

"This weather is Hell," Lindsay countered and we laughed as they pulled away. Henry blew me a kiss from the back seat.

Dinner was late that night. Remy and Lon were just sitting down. I was at the sink when I heard her voice, Lindsay, in our house, standing in the entry hall, calling my name. I rounded the corner expecting a usual request for an onion or milk or coffee for the morning; supplementing grocery gaps was a long-standing tradition on our street.

"Something bad happened," Lindsay said. Freja was standing next to her, even paler than usual. "There was an accident with Henry. He was playing near the electric gate at grandma's. He got his neck stuck in between it, in between the gate and the post where it seals shut." My hand covered my mouth like a shador, only my wide eyes visible. "It took them 20 minutes to come. I told them to bring the Jaws of Life. They didn't listen. Rach is at the ER with him now. I need to get Freja some dinner."

I focused on the only part of the story I had any control over. "Hey, Fray, what do you feel like? You want me to make you some pasta?" She nodded excitedly and Lindsay and I exchanged glances, grateful for the simple gift of comfort food. "Ok, why don't you guys go home? I'll make it and bring it over. Just butter and cheese, right, Fray?"

Freja nodded. She had seen the whole thing. Seen her brother in the grip of the gate while her mother held him weeping and praying, a woman who had gotten sober by believing in a Higher Power that she would often tell me could be a rock or a chair—it could be anything she wanted it to be—now praying to the Creator God, the God of Abraham and Isaac and Jacob, clutching Henry's limp, bluing body in her arms, like Mary holding Christ in the

Pieta, as his neck swelled between the cold, hard metal slats. "Oh God, Oh God, Oh God, she cried out. Save my son."

Our neighborhood family needed to know right away. I put water on the stove to boil and went across the street to Kelly and Scott's. Lon, with his 25 years of experience in following up on my abandoned household projects, took the lid off the pot before it exploded and poured the noodles in. I came back, hugged him, reminded him just butter and cheese, and went back outside, down the street five houses to Tina and Tim's.

The sky was ink and it was still well into the 90s. I was barefoot and wearing a dress that I got the year Bono released his Project (Red) collection of clothes to support famine relief in Africa. The material was like some breathable burlap that had been dyed in the hands of women who knelt by a riverbed singing; it made me feel the same way the air did, like every time I wore it, I was in my right House and floating. I walked down the middle of the street, the asphalt warm beneath my feet, and saw myself in a village somewhere, walking between the huts, singing God's praises, scooping out bowls of rice on my knees in the dirt and smiling. While others dreamed of overnight millions, my vision was of one day becoming selfless enough to be a light in the darkest corners.

I knocked several times before they answered, stood in their entry hall, destroyed the illusion that on this balmy fall night all was well: an hour before, Remy had been with Tina at a spinning class she taught at the Y. Now she stood with her husband, both of them cupping their hands over their mouths, as if the loss of breath from a blow like that

71

might lead to collapse. Their children, Keaton and Adelaide, played with Henry every single day. We hugged and wept and made sure everyone had everyone else's cell phone numbers before I went on to Dave and Amanda's and checked the houselights at Tom's.

Tom had known more suffering than most, his wife Veronika dying three years before, leaving their young children without a mother. She had had complications from the flu, went into the hospital to hydrate, never came home. Tom had delivered the news to me standing on the very same patch of my entry hall where I had just received the news about Henry. In the years since his wife died, Tom had lost his mother and his father and his closest friend. A devout Catholic, he believed in taking the knocks you were dealt, never missed a Mass, never let his kids miss one either. There's a village in Africa with a center that cares for HIV sufferers. It's called *Veronika's Place*. She had raised the funds in the final years of her life. It had been her passion, her pride, her Call. The parishioners at her church have kept it going, this gift of flesh and time and love, the house that Veronika built before she dissolved from flesh into spirit and left us here on the cul-de-sac, both poorer and richer.

We live in a world of hard surfaces, and when our children fall they hit things that God did not create. The children of Israel took their spills on dirt and sand. They did not need helmets to get through the day. Ours is a world of asphalt and steel, of things moving too fast to be tamed, of kids on wheels, on rooftops, on benders. The year I became a Christian, a teenaged girl from our church had been out with some friends doing what many teenagers do, pushing the limits, feeling new feelings. They had been surfing on the rooftop of a kid's car as he drove through the empty Costco parking lot at midnight, the air thick with the smell of In n' Out french fries. She hit head first. I heard that she was dead; later there was a correction: not dead, but nearly. Almost. Her brain badly damaged. She had been a straight-A student but all that accumulated knowledge was left splattered on the macadam. Now she wore a helmet to church and a vague expression that would stay there for years.

When the widow's young son became ill, she lashed out at Elijah: **"'What have you against me, O man of God? You have come to me to bring my sin to remembrance, and to cause the death of my son!'**

But [Elijah] said to her, 'Give me your son.' He took him from her bosom, carried him up into the upper chamber where he was lodging, and laid him on his own bed. He cried out to the LORD, 'O LORD my God, have you brought calamity even upon the widow with whom I am staying, by killing her son?'

Then he stretched himself upon the child three times, and cried out to the LORD, 'O LORD my God, let this child's life come into him again.'" (1 Kings 17:18-21)

As I walked barefoot on the warm asphalt to deliver the news of Henry's accident, I cried out to the LORD. I thought of this passage—the very passage I had arrived at through my own narrative the day before the accident. I lifted my arms up and pressed my hands on the top of my head, as if to contain the rising vapor of deliberation. If scripture were a living communication with God what, then—in this case so acutely timed and pointed—was I supposed to glean from it? Was I literally supposed to go to the hospital, to bend over his bedside, to splay myself across his chest in prayer? I wanted to dissolve into that, to be that; I wanted to run from that, to shoo it aside. No, He doesn't mean that really. He can't mean really. Not literally. I do not have a Gift for healing. Well, Elijah didn't either, not until that moment. He was a prophet; he was the guy who spent his time muttering in the woods broken up by great big moments of blowing the rulers and the masses away. But heal he did; in a pinch, God will use any willing vessel. But I could no more bring myself to drive over to UCLA and say to Rachel and her family, now gathered at his bedside, "excuse me, I just want to lay on top of your bruised son for a minute." I couldn't do it. Wouldn't do it. Prayed that the price of my weakness—or was it discernment?—would not be paid by him. As I stood in the middle of the street lit up in a halo of incandescent light, walking through the air where time stood still, I prayed the image of myself pressing my body across Henry's, breathing life into him, my heart against his, God's pulse upon him, three times I did it in my own mind's eye. I breathed in the scent of Henry's little boy flesh, felt his skin on my skin, the boy I had held every day since he was a baby. "Oh LORD my God, I cried. Save this boy." Then I opened my eyes and knocked on the next door.

Even in the midst of crisis, there is still the gnaw and tug of provision. With me writing yet another book and beginning to help Remy craft an independent education, I sensed in Lon a base level of fear—maybe a tinge of resentment—that there would be too much money going out, not enough coming in. Wouldn't be for a while. Two years prior, the month before we had both gotten laid off, I had a very strong sense that the economy was not headed in a good direction (I read the paper, too). I suggested to Lon that we rent out our back house, a sliver of a room that nonetheless had its own entrance and bath and TV: we could pick up a microwave and a mini fridge and take in a college student. He didn't like the idea at all. I persisted. A dear friend of mine from church (whose name also happens to be Rachel), was an executive at the post-graduate school at the RAND Corporation. She connected us with a young woman, a doctoral candidate, who moved in the month before we both got laid off and stayed with us for a year and a half; she planned to spend her final year of school in a slightly larger space.

On the day of Henry's accident, I had a strong sense that I should call her, see if she might want to come back at some point. I never got around to it, but the next morning, I got an email from her: the new house where she was supposed to be living had bed bugs. Was our place by any chance still available? Why, yes, by chance, it was. She moved in the next day, back for another year, slipping a check for $500 for the first month in the mailbox.

"Well, that's nothing to sneeze at," Lon said, smiling.

"No," I said, cryptically. "It's not."

Throughout the day, texts and emails and phone calls flew, carrying prayers from around the city straight to Henry's hospital bed, around Rachel's shoulders, around the house and the whole family. The school kids in Freja's class made a fat stack of brightly colored cards, each bursting with messages of love and hope and drawings of dinosaurs and flowers, each with a Bible verse or a snippet of Psalms. Rachel spread them out across his windowsill in the ICU as one after another possibility of every horrible thing—brain bleeds, brain damage, paralysis—fell by the wayside. Swollen and stubborn, Henry was non-responsive as the doctors tried to test his fine motor, his gross motor, his cognition. Jonas, his father, set an iPad in front of Henry's purple, bloated face. Like a reflex he reached out his four-year old finger and began to type his name on the virtual keys to access his favorite game.

"The Lord listened to the voice of Elijah; the life of the child came into him again, and he revived. Elijah took the child, brought him down from the upper chamber into the house, and gave him to his mother: then Elijah said, 'See, your son is alive.' So the woman said to Elijah, 'Now I know that you are a man of God, and that the word of the LORD in your mouth is truth.'" (1 Kings 17:22-24)

Forty-eight hours after his head and neck had been pressed to the point of crushing between the motorized forces of an old automated gate, Henry was home, surrounded by neighbors, playing with his friends in the back yard—gentle, guys, gentle—his prayer cards reposted around his room. On her Facebook page his mother wrote, *This is a miracle. A miracle. I will say it again. A miracle.*

Chapter 6

Graham was born tall and lean like me. He was 5' 10'/135 lbs. when they put him on the Varsity Baseball team at 13. The Coach told me to have him eat a big bowl of cereal each night before bed to fatten him up. Instead, I served up giant bowls of instant mashed potatoes with whole sticks of butter until he nearly choked on them. Graham didn't have much of an appetite, particularly during the school year when the rush and stress of classes and practice and homework left him feeling tight in the gut most days. He liked a little yogurt and fruit for breakfast. I'd make him a PB & J every morning and find a half dozen of them molding in his backpack at month's end.

In his junior year, Graham was invited to some of the most prestigious scouting camps in the nation, invitation-only, fully-hosted showcases at Pepperdine and UCLA and Irvine. John Savage, the Bruin coach, called him by name when he arrived, now 6' 1 and 155 lbs. His bio read 175, an optimistic fudge on the part of his high school coach. On the morning of his all-day try-out with the UCLA program, Graham didn't want to eat. I forced him. Made him a plate of bacon and eggs and toast, a real breakfast of champions. He choked down what he could and got in the car.

There was a mist over the field as Graham and the rest of the 50 hand-selected players began to jog, the parents nervously sizing up their comparative gaits. The players were broken into groups to be tested on a range of skills: foot speed, hand speed, bat speed. Graham's group was timed in the 100-yard dash, two times each. From up in the stands there was no way to know how he'd done, but his body language spoke volumes: his hands were on his hips and his head was bowed slightly. I leaned forward, as if drawing even a few inches closer would give me a better sense of what was going on a field away. His group was rotated to the drill at first base. Graham appeared to be hanging back. I rose, began to inch down the stadium seats. He was now standing on the foul line just beyond first base, hands on his knees, head dropped half way to the ground and, suddenly, heaving. A few minutes later, the trainer reported back to me that, after throwing up, Graham had opted to withdraw from the morning exercises, which meant withdrawing from consideration as an outfielder. He had chosen to rest in the dugout and save his strength for pitching, his primary position.

By the time Graham took to the mound, he looked strong and confident. Each of the dozen or so pitchers were given an inning. Graham got the only pick-off of the day, struck out another, got the third to ground out to short. He looked good. They all did. They weren't there by chance. But there was one young man who stood out above all the strapping young pitching gods. His name was Rob Rasmussen. He was only 5"8" and as lean as Graham. He struck out every batter, 1-2-3. Had a curve and a change-up that kept them guessing and a fastball fast enough to do the trick. He was given a second inning, then a third: down they went, nine of the best power hitters in the state, felled by this boy so physically unimpressive that it would not be hard to imagine him hung by his belt loops in a bathroom stall at school. He slayed them all that day and all through his early years at UCLA, who recruited him on the spot. Four years later, Graham and I watched Rob Rasmussen pitch in the College World Series, then get picked up as a junior in the second round of the MLB draft, a little bit thicker, an inch or two taller—but still the same slight, devastatingly effective lefty we remembered from that day. Gifts often come in unexpected packages.

I stopped forcing Graham to eat more than his appetite demanded after that. If God wanted him to play baseball in college then whatever had to kick in would. Or not. He knew who he was. The time spent alone on the mound reveals and defines character in much the same way as the time spent alone on the ice does for a figure skater. In those few charged moments, when the music plays and the judges make their marks, no amount of wishful thinking or expensive training can compensate for the child who does not have the personal tools to make adjustments, regroup, stand tall, and carry on. And the only conceivable way to develop these tools is to struggle and to fail.

The attempt to prevent our kids from struggling for fear it might scar their permanent records is, instead, scarring them for life. The statistics are alarming. Even the best and the brightest, the ones who manage to jump through all the right hoops in exactly the right time sequence, the ones who are supposed to have it made— don't. Cases of college students seeking therapy, anti-depressants, emotional escape of all kinds are at an all-time high. Incidents of straight-A students running out of steam two years into college have become commonplace. Pining for the simple adolescent days they gave away to cramming, striving, not disappointing, they try to recapture them with binge drinking or rebellion by mediocrity. Those who do earn their degrees are moving home in record numbers, unable to find jobs, or at least jobs that live up to the expectations that their perfect track records have instilled in them. Their parents hover, wondering where it all went wrong, how they failed to get the most out of their investment: all the tutors, all the extracurriculars, all that college tuition, and now, like milk-fed veal, their offspring sit, glued to their laptops, their ear buds, their visions of entitlement, unable to figure out what comes next or how the world could deny them their due.

"What have you against me, O man of God? You have come to me to bring my sin to remembrance, and to cause the death of my son!" (1 Kings 17:18)

This is what the widow said to Elijah when she first discovered her son was dying. It feels like an antiquated notion, the idea that we are punished for our sins. Contemporary ears often reject the very concept of sin, shoving it into the attic of our minds with images like blood letting, and the plague, and notions of a flat earth. But sin—

no less than blood and breath and DNA—lives on in the heart of man, whether we acknowledge it or not. The best description I ever heard was shared by both St. Augustine and Martin Luther, who characterized sin as *Homo Incurvatus in Se*: Man Turned in on Himself. We turn—away from others, leaving ourselves isolated and despairing. We turn in—obsessing on our own perceived needs, blocking our view of greater rewards. We turn in on ourselves—our very flesh and fiber becoming like Pac-Men that devour our hopes of ever becoming whole. Paul's excruciating confession in his letter to the early believers in Rome says it all: **"I do not understand my own actions. For I do not do what I want, but I do the very thing I hate ... Now if I do what I do not want to do, it is no longer I who do it, but sin that dwells within me."** (Romans 7:15,19-20)

The same truth is echoed in the Gospel of St. Matthew (26:41): **"...the spirit indeed is willing, but the flesh is weak."**

The Elijah passage never indicates what the widow's sin was. Maybe her son was the child of adultery. Maybe she treated her servants cruelly. Maybe she gossiped maliciously at the gate where Elijah first met her. Who knows? What is curious is that Elijah never brings it up, never accuses her of anything. It is the mother who confesses, the mother who feels it bubble up in her gut, the connection between something going wrong with her child and some flaw in herself. It is the mother who knows—primordial, womb-fed knowing—that these things can only be addressed by God.

And addressed they were. Once the widow had been reminded of the full breadth and depth of God's power through the resurrection of her son—the first human resurrection in recorded history—it was time for her to let Elijah go on to even bigger things. God told him so in no uncertain terms.

"Go, [now], present yourself to Ahab; I will send rain on the earth. So Elijah went to present himself to Ahab." (1 Kings 18:1)

At this point, the story takes on a bit of a sitcom feel. Picture this: just as Elijah is journeying from Zerephath to Samaria to present himself to Ahab, Ahab and Obadiah, his palace chief and secret servant of the LORD, are planning a Hail-Mary journey of their own.

"Ahab said to Obadiah, 'Go through the land to all the springs of water, and to all the wadis; perhaps we may find grass to keep the horses and mules alive, and not lose some of the animals.'

So they divided the land between them to pass through it; Ahab went in one direction by himself, and Obadiah went in another direction by himself." (1 Kings 18:5-6)

I picture these three—Elijah, Ahab, Obadiah—all walking around the desert to the soundtrack of *Peter and the Wolf*...Duh, duh, duh, dun dun dun... First off, we have the king of all of Israel now walking around by himself looking for scraps of dried grass to save his horses. Why? Well, we know why he wants to save his horses, as opposed to, say, some of his people—he's a pig. But why is *he* the one looking for the last of the resources when surely he has hundreds of men—soldiers, servants, field hands with no fields to tend—who could be doing this for him? Has he lost trust in them? Or they in him? His crown slipping on his sweaty brow, dust choking his throat as he moves through the brush, Ahab searches in vain.

Meanwhile, a few miles away, in another wide open patch of parched land, ...Duh, duh, duh, dun, dun, dun... Obadiah, who has been a servant of the LORD since his youth—who has secretly hidden 100 of the LORD's prophets from the blood-thirsty queen and kept them alive all through the drought—runs into Elijah. It would be as if Rahm Emmanuel were to meet face to face with that guy you tried to avoid at the mall last weekend, the one standing on a box shouting *Jesus Saves*. As you can imagine, they do not greet as equals. Instantly, Obadiah, in his palace finery, drops to his knees before the prophet: **"Is it you, my lord Elijah?" He answered him, "It is I. Go, tell your lord that Elijah is here."** (1 Kings 18:7-8)

In the junior year of high school, American college-bound students are expected to take not only the SAT but a selection of SAT Subject exams to prove their competency in particular fields. Graham, having gotten a B in Chemistry, figured he'd have a shot at a halfway decent score. His preparation was, as far as I knew, quite good. Venice High was highly regarded for its science programs; they even won a National Science Bowl title one year. When the results arrived, I squinted in disbelief. Was that a 1? Had he actually come out in the lowest percentile in the nation for students who had taken this test? How was that even possible? Didn't they give you like 5% just for showing up? How could someone with a 96th percentile IQ get a score that was tantamount to leaving every answer blank? If he had been a different kind of kid, I might have wondered if he'd slipped out the back door of the classroom, skipped the exam altogether.

On the other hand, there's our friend, Matt. His family goes to our church. The parents are both educated and faithful people; the father is a psychologist. His son was a few years older than Graham, and I often asked how life was for him at Venice High. The father told me that there were challenges. That Matt had been struggling with some depression and other issues. That his grades had suffered. One semester he had to take a sabbatical. I wondered what sort of life would come next for him after stepping out of the race just when it counted most. Next thing I knew, Matt was heading off to Berkeley. I asked his dad how it was possible that his son's grades had suffered so much, that he missed a whole semester of his junior year, and that he still was admitted to a school as selective as any of the Ivy League.

"He got a perfect score on his SAT Subject exam in Chemistry," he told me. "They just waived him in."

So here they are, two young men raised from youth under the wings of the LORD, each with different gifts, different paths. Would Matt ever wish to be like Graham? Did Graham ever wish he were more like Matt? Do we parents who rip open the test results—academic, medical—

wish in those moments that our children had different gifts? Different challenges?

What about Obadiah and Elijah? Would Obadiah have given anything for one day as a true prophet? One day to feel the full force of that power surging through his veins? Would Elijah have given up a few of his miracles for a more comfortable life in the palace? To love the LORD from a safe distance? What about their mothers? Are we really honest with ourselves when we say all we want is for our children to be happy, or do we all suffer, to varying degrees, from grass-is-always-greener syndrome? And if so, what do we do—what will our children do— when all the grass in the land dries up?

I had always thought that the American Dream was a colloquial extension of our Constitution, our rightful quest for life, liberty, and the pursuit of happiness, unfettered. This seems to be the spirit in which the idea was first expressed by James Truslow Adams in 1931:

"Life should be better and richer and fuller for everyone, with opportunity for each according to ability or achievement ... It is not a dream of motor cars and high wages merely, but a dream of social order in which each man and each woman shall be able to attain to the fullest stature of which they are innately capable and be recognized by others for what they are, regardless of the fortuitous circumstances of birth or position."

It was a beautiful dream, deeply rooted in Judeo-Christian theology and the innate right of human beings to self-actualize. Naturally, we gilded the lily until it hung so heavy on the branch as to snap it right from the root. By the middle of the 20th century, the American Dream had developed a new and singular benchmark: home ownership. To own one's own home, to do gratifying work—preferably not with one's hands—to send one's kids to college so that they could own their own homes and find their own work—nothing manual, certainly—this was the new American Dream. The other night I heard a news commentator reference the phrase rhetorically. "That's what the American Dream is all about, right? The expectation that each generation will do better than their parents." No one even blinked. The part about being "recognized by others for what they are" has been long forgotten.

America is a young country, young and brash and prone to errors. Like teenagers. For all our inherent goodness, we've been cursed with bright, shiny object disease and we don't want a cure. Not now. Not till we get our little taste, till our kids get theirs. But the kingdom of God wasn't born yesterday. Corruption and greed and the love of evil are old news to Him. When the time is right, when the landscape is dry, when palaces fail to meet our deepest needs, we may be ready to listen once again.

Ed Rosenthal was not a religious man. An L.A. real estate broker who just sold his first property in over a year, he wanted to celebrate with a hike through his favorite National Park in Joshua Tree. He loved the desert, was drawn to its spiritual qualities. **"The desert will lead you to your heart where I will speak,"** said the ancient prophet Hosea (2:16). Modern day prophets, U2, named their fifth album *The Joshua Tree* as a witness to the "spiritual drought" they saw in this country, and a testament to "those on the fringes of the promised land, cut off from the American Dream."

Ed Rosenthal had hiked the trails of Joshua Tree many times before. He took a small emergency kit with him but only a pint of water. A careless oversight. A foolish error. The warm currents had begun to move in across Southern California, the same sweltering system that would hold a thousand prayers for my neighbor Henry. It was well into the 90s the Friday Ed set out, and before he knew it, he'd lost his way. Hour after hour he stumbled across canyons, through brush, his mouth turning to sand, his saliva to gravel. The nights were cold and he wrapped himself in a space blanket and tucked his diminishing body beneath the shelter of a broom tree. By Monday he was certain he would die. He began to write notes to his wife and daughter on his sweat-stained cap. He told them he loved them. He told them whom to trust for financial advice. He told them that he wanted his wake to be "a drunken, joyous party with Persian food."

Ed Rosenthal was not a religious man, but his parents had seen to it that he went to Hebrew school. He'd learned the Torah. He'd learned the *Shema Yisrael*, the central prayer of Judaism. Although he'd spent his life as a secular Jew, the words were still there, buried under layers of sinewy self-reliance now taut with worry over escrow accounts and land development deals and commission checks that failed to appear. On his knees in the desert, his tongue dry as the Santa Ana winds, he cried out in his native Hebrew:

"Hear, O Israel: The LORD is our God, the LORD alone. You shall love the LORD your God with all your heart, and with all your soul, and with all your might.

Keep these words that I am commanding you today in your heart. Recite them to your children and talk about them when you are at home and when you are away, when you lie down and when you rise.

Bind them as a sign on your hand, fix them as an emblem on your forehead, and write them on the doorposts of your house and on your gates." (Deuteronomy, 6:4-9)

When he was done, he prayed for rain. Ten seconds later, the rain came, piercing the drought in fat, merciful droplets. Ed Rosenthal fell on his back and lapped at the gift and marveled at the greatness of a God he had long stopped believing in. "It was definitely a miracle," he said. He lasted six days without food and water before being rescued and restored to perfect health. Speaking to reporters a week later he said, "My conclusion is that God is real. Really. I have to tell you. God is real."

I am fascinated by the Jewish practice of Shabbat. I read with great interest of the growing movement of young Jewish families, mostly Orthodox, but some Reform, who actually practice this very real, present and physical act of living out their faith in contemporary life. Each Friday night before sundown they finish preparing their meals for the next 24 hours so they can turn off the stove, the lights, themselves. They light candles and prepare to greet friends, where, free from the hustle and rush, they eat and pray and laugh and enjoy this gift, Life. There are no smart phones at the table. No texts stealing attention from loved ones. There is peace in the home, peace in mind and spirit, peace of the LORD in the House of His people. **"The Sabbath was made for humankind, and not humankind for the Sabbath."** (Mark 2:27). Come Sunday those same people will be driving and shopping and cheering their children on at soccer games, but they will not be quite the same, each Sabbath renewing them for the week again, solidifying their ties to the God of Abraham and Isaac and Jacob.

My own devotional life is born of ancient practices, as well. I begin each day with a method of prayer called *lectio divina*, or divine reading, in which you read scripture the way a blind person might read Braille: slowly, mindfully, feeling the bumps and curves of each word and phrase, until something leaps out. This is God's word for you that day, the very thing He is trying to communicate to you, your daily bread. This is the living God relating to you personally as you sit in a parked car or a cubicle or a line at the DMV. Often times the importance of the word or phrase is unclear, but when you let it sink in deeply, prayerfully, when you ask for its richness to be opened, it feeds you.

So often when we speak of voices and instructions from God it sounds like a literal thing, but most times, for me at least, it's not. I usually hear from God in a few different ways. Sometimes I see things, images, impressions, visions—like a billboard across my mind's eye. That's the big, cool stuff that propels me forward, shows me how and what to create, to throw myself into. For the day-to day bugaboos, the struggles with fear or doubt or anger or sloth, the answers usually come (and none too quickly) in a gentle understanding of something not previously understood, a pressing in of insight, always calm, never shrill. If I hear a loud voice shouting I know it's just my own ego being bossy, trying to control what is not mine to control. Or worse, the enemy trying to distract me. But the most common way that God speaks to me is through people.

"The candle was out at church again," Remy told me one day when I picked her up at school. She was 10. "The red one that hangs in the corner."

"The eternal flame, you mean?"

She had mentioned it more than once. "It sounds like maybe God has a job for you."

"What do you mean?" she asked.

"Well, every chapel there're over 100 kids there. And every Sunday over 250 adults. But you're the only one who keeps noticing that the candle's gone out. Or at least the only one who's been bothered enough by it to mention it. Sounds to me like you're the one God wants to give the job to."

And so for two years, once a week after school, we would walk into the church together and bow at the altar. I would position the ladder and Remy would hold it steady as I stepped up to remove the lamp. Back in the sacristy, we'd take out the jug of oil and, with a child's breathless reverence, Remy would hold the funnel as I poured. When the lamp was wiped clean, we'd light the wick anew and return it to the hanging stand in the sanctuary as a testament: Remy had listened to God and I had listened to Remy, and that, we both came to understand, as the small single flame transformed the dark red glass to a bright, warm glow, was how we were intended to keep the eternal flame burning. Selah.

Graham went off to California State University at Long Beach at 17. He began to eat well and thrive, gaining 20 pounds his first year. His shoulders took on the look of the athlete he no longer was and it was impossible for me not to think *Now you get these shoulders?* He got involved in a fraternity—a new band of brothers—took on leadership roles, declared a major in journalism. He got hired for an internship at a local paper, starting off with sports coverage, moving on, the following summer, to a $23-an-hour internship in the corporate communications department of one of the nation's largest and most progressive private utility companies. He was recruited by Long Beach Poly High School—*Sports Illustrated* dubbed it "The Sports School of the Century"—as the head coach of their JV baseball team, a paid position that made him responsible, at the age of 19, for 20 kids and two assistant coaches, one of them over twice his age. Meanwhile, his sports writing blossomed into a knack for writing of all kinds and, just before his 21st birthday, he was made the Editor-in-Chief of *Dig*, the Long Beach State magazine, a job which involves recruiting, training, and supervising a staff of student freelancers.

Not a day of his baseball playing was wasted, not a moment of chasing that dream. In an age where we demand a return on investment for every breath, here lies the only true promise of ROI:

"As the rain and the snow come down from heaven, and do not return to it without watering the earth and making it bud and flourish, so that it yields seed for the sower and bread for the eater, so is my word that goes out from my mouth. It will not return to me empty, but will accomplish what I desire and achieve the purpose for which I sent it." (Isaiah 55:10-11)

Chapter 7

Ok, so here's what happens next. That wacko on the milk crate with the dreadlocks in the mall—you know, the one who is either a prophet or a madman or both—well, he marches onto the trading floor of the NYSE wearing a soiled *Here Comes Trouble* t-shirt and starts telling all the wing-tippers what's what. "You," he says, "you started all this, but now God's gonna finish it. Call all the nation. Meet me at the top of Mount Rushmore. Bring all the false prophets—the hedge fund managers, the violent game makers, the gun pushers, the sports agents, the plastic surgeons, the mortgage brokers, the size-2 dress designers, the porn producers, the corrupt CEOs, the silent partners, and the elected officials who sold their souls—assemble them all for me. Now! And without batting an eye, the all-powerful start jumping through hoops to oblige the deranged man whom they have no choice but to believe might be able to save them.

Ok, so that was the remake. Here's the original: **"When Ahab saw Elijah, Ahab said to him, 'Is it you, you troubler of Israel?' He answered, 'I have not troubled Israel; but you have, and your father's house,** because you have forsaken the commandments of the LORD and followed the Baals.'

'Now therefore have all Israel assemble for me at Mount Carmel, with the four hundred fifty prophets of Baal and the four hundred prophets of Asherah, who eat at Jezebel's table.'" (1 Kings 18:17-19)

Consider Ahab's desperation. The day before, he was out scavenging his own land for scraps of grass. Now, in front of everyone in the palace, he is accused of being the source of all of Israel's problems and is being ordered around by a prophet of the God he has directed his people to turn away from. Ahab doesn't even bother to say, "Now wait just a minute there, bub." He doesn't ask the guards to remove the intruder. He doesn't attempt to discredit Elijah or his claims. The time for posturing is over. Without help and the promise of rain, they will all soon be dead. And despite his prodigal, pagan ways, Ahab knows—we all know—that when it comes to matters of life and death, there's no where else to turn but God. In an act of pure self-preservation, he orders the kingdom to convene to hear what Elijah has to say. And Elijah, true to form, minces no words: **"How long will you go limping with two different opinions? If the LORD is God, follow him; but if Baal, then follow him." The people did not answer him a word."** (1 Kings 18:21)

We are a have-your-cake-and-eat-it-too people. We want to treat ourselves to our little sins and not feel bad about it. We want to believe in angels but have no interest in affiliating them with anything other than a generic fairy-dusted light. We love candles and incense and a filmy sense of warmth and things that glow beyond the edges, but the narrative? The plot is so outdated, so 3rd world. And the characters? Oh, how we howl at the notion that evil might have a commander in chief. We love Christmas presents but not Christ, Easter baskets but not crosses. We want to tell our friends with cancer that we will pray for them (we don't) and our puddle-eyed children that their goldfish have gone to heaven (doubtful). When we lose our jobs we want to take comfort in the idea that God doesn't give us more than we can handle, but really, how can we? We have absolutely no idea what God has given us or what it might be for. We haven't talked to Him in ages.

Ten years ago, my former pastor, Pastor Ken, challenged the whole congregation on New Year's Day. Make this the year you read *The Bible* cover to cover. If you block out a half hour a day you'll be finished in a year and your life will be changed forever. Many nodded their heads ambitiously, filled out good-intention cards. By March my friend Barbara and I were the only two left. We had come to the church a few years apart, come to faith as worldly adults. Barbara is a gifted artist, has her BFA from Scripps, oversees one of the largest personal art collections in the country. She and her husband co-own and manage two of the trendiest, hippest, call-six-weeks-in-advance restaurants in Venice, ground zero for cool. God's people are everywhere.

"Oh my gosh," I said to Barb in one of our many support calls that year. "Slogging through Numbers is just Hell. All those names. All those rules. I'm dying!"

We would try to encourage those who were falling by the wayside. "You just have to gut it out through those early books; just push through all the dust and the detail. If you stop now you'll just die in the desert and never make it. Keep going. It gets better. Really."

The duller and less relevant it felt the more determined we were to stick with it: on bad days we doubled our reading time. Through the Pentateuch, through Joshua and Judges and Samuel and Kings 1 & 2, through Job and the Psalms, the Proverbs and the prophets, all the way up to the New Testament, to the Gospel, to Matthew, Mark, Luke and John, where we could feel the weight of the Law lift and the windows open, and the curtains brush against our cheeks in the breeze.

"Oh my gosh," Barb said one morning, calling me on her bluetooth on the way in to work. "I just got the whole part about the Holy Spirit. Unbelievable. I mean, I never really got how that worked and then…oh my gosh, this is so cool!"

It was a great year. A remarkable year. I could have finished up before Christmas, but wanted the discipline of the daily reading to see me through till the very end. On New Year's Eve day, Remy had a friend over. Usually I read my Bible in private, in a tattered old chair in my bedroom, alone, with the door closed. But on this day I brought my big, red Bible—*The New Oxford Annotated*—and plopped myself down smack in the middle of the living room. I opened to the final pages of Revelation and cleared my throat. I could hear the girls in the kitchen, giggling, then hushed. They ran in and out of the room, looking over each time, pausing. Finally, I read and savored the last, last words, **"The grace of the Lord Jesus be with all the saints. Amen."** And closed the book. Not quietly.

"Well, that's that," I said, stretching out my arms for affect. "I just finished reading the entire Bible."

Remy's friend went wide-eyed, drew closer. With all the sincerity in her nine-year old heart she said, "So now you understand everything?"

How can you possibly explain to a child that the more you know, the more you realize you know very little indeed. Instead, I smiled and said what was, in fact, the truth. "Yep," I told her. "Now I understand everything."

Barbara has one son, Kyle, who is life and breath and sustenance to her. It was because of Kyle that we came into each other's lives. She had brought him to our little church school in Venice as a five-year old and within moments he turned to her beaming, "This is it, mom. This is my school!" She, like me, was a believer in listening to your kid's deepest instincts.

Kyle was a great student, a great athlete, a great friend. He was the all-American boy, strapping and happy and full of life. He left First Lutheran School a straight-A student and went off to a Catholic high school in Santa Monica. He loved it there, so much so that suddenly he was not such a great student anymore. Barb would call me on the phone wailing.

"He got a D on his report card. He's never gotten a D in his life!"

I reminded her that high school was different. That lots of kids get Ds at first and then learn to dig out of their holes. Kyle was also a baseball player with dreams of playing in college. We watched as they jumped through many of the same hoops that we had with Graham. We tried to share what we knew without dampening any of their enthusiasm: who knew, maybe it would be different for him. Kyle had what parents with an eye on college would call a disastrous sophomore year: more Cs than As, as I recall. In his junior year, he seemed to be plagued with the same resistance that I had seen in Graham; they balked at having to spell out the meaning of life in neat little essays for others to read, approve, judge, compare. "What is the author saying? What is the author feeling?" Graham used moan as he mocked his Honors English assignments. "If they want to know so badly, why don't they ask the author?"—this from a boy who is now a man who sees the writing of books as well within his wheelhouse.

Barb thanked God that Kyle was a good test taker. He got a solid score on his first SAT and an even better one on his second. He spent weekends going to college baseball clinics, trying to envision a future built around that perfect green diamond. As the final months the application season drew to a close, he thought increasingly of New Mexico, his mother's home state. Every year, they would take Kyle there to visit family. Every year, I heard stories about how much he loved it, the landscape, the cousins, how he felt in his skin when he was there. He sent his baseball stats to the coach at University of New Mexico, tried to make it all come together. If the coach was considering Kyle in any way, he hid it well. Kyle picked UNM anyway, and they packed up the car in August.

"Wait!" his dad shouted. He ran back into the house to grab Kyle's glove and cleats, tried to shove them in the back of the overstuffed car.

"There's no room," Kyle said, without a hint of sadness, and just like that, left them behind.

Within a week he was calling home babbling enthusiastically about becoming a Business Major and taking French and running a triathalon with his cousin in December. Kyle was in his new House and all was right with the world. All the angst and the misery and the shouting and the wringing of hands over this grade or that, this score or that, this batting average or that, was all just an exercise that ages parents but rarely changes a child's destiny.

"Therefore I tell you, do not worry about your life, what you will eat or what you will drink, or about your body, what you will wear. Is not life more than food and the body more than clothing? ... And can any of you by worrying add a single hour to your span of life?" (Matthew 6:25, 27)

But I do worry about America's boys. They are dropping out of high school at alarming rates, and contributing to a shift in college demographics that would have been unheard of even two decades ago. The average college campus in the U.S. is now nearly 60% female. As a woman I imagine this is supposed to make me feel proud, excited, vindicated. But as a member of a society peopled with young men, I mourn for them. I don't think it's the material they can't handle, but the relentless scheduling and monitoring of strategic, time-sensitive goals so out of keeping with most boys' natural temperaments. Girls, for the most part, love to make little to-do lists, to jot them out in purple pen in their best cursive with a heart at the end of the tasks they deem most special. They love to work their way through those lists and cross them off with a smack of their glossed lips. Long-term planning is a gift born of estrogen, of the knowledge that every 28 days is a matter of life and death. Boys, by nature, live in the moment. At a time when we ask them to declare what they want to do with the rest of their lives, all they're thinking about is what they're going to have for lunch and if the throb in their bodies will ever be relieved in an acceptable manner; they want to laugh and jostle and feel mighty and herd buffalo and we want them to sit very still for long periods of time and think. Hard. As if their lives depended on it. We drill and drill and drill about four-year college, that it's that or death, that or homelessness. That the world will leave them behind if they don't agree to keep sitting in these same stupefying classrooms for years and years more. So much of it feels pointless, even for the girls, but the girls still like to please. The boys, at an increasing rate, are saying take your A-G requirements and shove 'em.

Many of them will be just fine, will settle down at the eleventh hour, get themselves into some kind of college and start growing up. Some of these boys will skip the college route, train to do good, necessary things, provide for families, walk their kids to school in the mornings, pack their lunches and love their wives, who will likely be the primary breadwinners. But many will be destroyed by the message of only one right path, by our failure to allow them to grow at their own rate, in their own way, in a direction that in some way colludes with the still, small voice in their dear, manchild hearts. We, as a nation, have committed the sin of overlaying quarterly earnings report thinking on God's precious works in progress, and whether in our own homes or our neighborhoods or our workforces or the tax load we are asked to bear, we will all pay the price.

Which brings us back to Elijah as he spells out the terms of the duel: a red state/blue state, pro everything/no everything, coffeehouse/tea party, my way or the highway, rubber-meets-the-road showdown the likes of which the world had never known: **"Let two bulls be given to us: let them [the 450 prophets of Baal] choose one bull for themselves, cut it in pieces and lay it on the wood, but put no fire to it; I will prepare the other bull and lay it on the wood, but put no fire to it."**

"Then you call on the name of your god and I will call on the name of the LORD; the god who answers by fire is indeed God.'"

"All the people answered, 'Well spoken!'" (1 Kings 17:23-24)

I saw the movie *Waiting for Superman* last week. The documentary captures the stories of passionate people giving their lives to reform the disaster of our American public education system. You won't hear a single person in the movie speaking about allowing kids to find their own paths. There is one path. College—and everyone's going, and everyone will be wholly prepared and everyone will feel worthy of the accomplishment. Brilliant vision. I pray each day for the people in that movie and those in the trenches who have made the educating and empowering of disregarded children their vocation. And yet, I see just as keenly the destructive power of turning education into a competitive sport.

So where does that leave us? If raising the bar of expectations to raise up the bottom echelon of students, families, and wage earners is psychologically and emotionally crippling middle-and-upper class children who are being forced to overachieve just to stay in the game, what does that mean for the common good? Do we simply need to accept the fact that this much-needed correction will likely shift the suffering to a new demographic for a while? That as the bottom rises, and other cultures bring new values to the table, that the privileged few may just need to scoot over? Or could it be that in God's capable hands, a reorganization of young destinies could be a blessing not only for the greater good, but for each and every individual child; a win-win-win times 10 billion souls? Just imagine a God's-eye view of the world, like one of those crazy-busy, computer-generated photo mosaics. Pull back far enough—the Ultimate aerial view—and we would be able to see clearly that He has no use for one-size-fits-all solutions, but rather weaves us together with a dizzying array of custom paths, each one of us in our right House, each one of our kids being guided—through doors that close as well as open—towards a call that will feed their minds, their spirit, their children. I like to think of all the tiny pixels of our collective lives forming a giant smiley face, at which, upon completion, God will wink and take His rest. It could happen. It really could. The grand tapestry with every thread in place, creating Heaven on earth in the hearts and lives of all its people. Can you even fathom the YouTube hits on that one?

There is one hitch, though. For all the pieces to fit together we'd all have to agree to abide by the vision—the master plan of the purpose of each of our respective lives—and play our small part in the big picture—Uhoh, small part, you say? That sounds like commie talk to me. Can't have that. We're Americans and if there's one thing Americans don't abide, it's anyone telling us what we can or can't do. No one puts Baby in a corner, am I right?

Case in point: the phenomenon of the Advanced Placement program. Begun in 1955, these courses were born out of a pilot study conducted at three East Coast prep schools certain that their best and brightest—students in the top 2 percentiles—needed a more challenging curriculum and should be allowed to start earning credits towards college. Didn't hurt the schools' recruiting pitches either. As with the SATs, everything snowballed from there. Because an AP class is worth an extra GPA point, they have become a *de facto* requirement for any aspiring college student. Earn a C, it shows up as a B. Earn an A, you'll get a 5.0. Before you know it, you have teen chat forums plagued with pained queries such as the one from a girl at a large public high school in Texas. After earning a 4.2 GPA, she's baffled and despondent to discover that her impressive academic record did not even earn her a spot in the top 25% in class rank and was well below the number to qualify her for a state scholarship. As you know, I'm no math whiz, but I'm pretty sure that numbers like these indicate that more than just the top 2% of students are taking the APs.

It's not hard to imagine how it came to this. The APs were designed for 98th percentile kids, so, of course, in comes the mom of a kid who's only in the 96th percentile, but she knows that her kid is just as smart and signs him up. The next year, it's the 94 percents and the 92 percents. A decade later, every mom of a perfectly bright, happy, wonderful kid who tests in the 80th percentile is certain that her child is just not being challenged enough, that he's clamoring for more. (Never met an 80th percentile kid who was clamoring for more work in high school, but I'm sure they're out there). And then it's the 70th percentile kids—their parents—scrambling to keep their sons and daughters from looking now, through no fault of their own, as if they're drifting back rather than edging up. You can't compete against kids who are getting an extra point for every class: even the 40th percentile kids can see that. So it's AP or die, even if your kid is not so academically gifted as to get anything out of the work. That's beside the point. Learning is no longer the goal. If it were we would not so blithely overlook the fact that 43% of high school students fail their year-end AP exams, earning 1s or 2s on a scale of 5. All we know—all anyone has to know—is that according to their transcripts, they are academic superstars.

I had never even heard of AP classes until a year before Graham started high school. Naively, I proclaimed at the start of his freshman year that I'd let him take one once he got to be a junior. His counselor told me differently. If he didn't take at least one AP class every year of high school, and preferably two or three, he could forget about even the UCs. Denial of the obvious is rampant: the 100% system is a zero-sum game. We can't fit more than 10% of the population into the 90th percentile no matter how hard we try. When a school has a mercilessly low acceptance rate, it is not a matter of opinion but a statistical certainty that we are setting our kids up for failure. And when those rejected have done every single thing right, everything that's been asked of them, demanded of them, they will have no choice but to imagine that their shortcoming is in some elusive "it" factor, not based on achievement but, rather, entirely personal. Something about them, something that is not quite up to snuff.

Back in the day when most Americans still behaved as if they believed that God made the world and everything in it, and that each child was precious in His sight, there was no such thing as Baby Einstein, or Music in Utero, speed reading or the Suzuki method; kids did more playing than homework, and some were A students and some were B students and some were C students and they all went on to play a part in adult lives that were considered some of the best, most productive years in American history. In the kingdom of God, percentiles are not limited to a narrow, vertical, zero-sum ladder, but expand up and out in all directions, creating openings like the secret gates in the train station that led to Hogwarts, allowing, say, a 27th percentile child to lead a perfectly wonderful, turbulent, blessed 99th percentile life. Sometimes, we need to look at the numbers in a new way.

Writing this chapter, I came across a handout that Graham had gotten from a history teacher once at Venice High. I had saved it all these years. It was created by scholar, Tim Wallace, at the University of California at Berkeley in 1996. Entitled *World Village*, it asks us to imagine shrinking the Earth's population down to 100 people, with all the ratios remaining the same. Here is what we would look like:

57 Asians, 21 Europeans, 14 from Western Hemisphere, 8 African
70 would be non-white; 30 would be white
70 would be non-Christian; 30 would be Christian
50% of the world's wealth would be in the hands of 6 people; all of these 6 people would be from the United States.
70 would be unable to read
50 would suffer from malnutrition
80 would live in substandard housing
1 would have a college education

The compassionate humanist in me sees the suffering and the poverty and knows that We the People are not paying attention to the right numbers. I hearken back to the words of best-selling author and psychiatrist, M. Scott Peck, who popularized the thinking of theologian Frederick Buechner when he explained that we would each find our true selves where "the world's deep need meets our deep joy." Hence, the urgency of teaching our children to listen for their Calls.

But the pragmatic logician in me notes something else entirely: if only one of the hundred has a college education, not only does that mean that we are overemphasizing the value of college, but that five out of the six wealthiest people in the world do not have college degrees. Bill Gates, Steve Jobs, Mark Zuckerberg—most of us know about these successful drop-outs by now, but what about Carl Bernstein, Billy Beane, Ansel Adams, Woody Allen, Ray Bradbury, James Cameron, Tom Carvel, Coco Chanel, Lee Clow, Dorothy Day, Ellen DeGeneres, Michael Dell, Richard DeVos, Walt Disney, Joe Dimaggio, Clint Eastwood, Larry Ellison, Debbie Fields, Bobby Fischer, F. Scott Fitzgerald, Dick Francis, Robert Frost, Buckminster Fuller, J.B. Fuqua, Lady Gaga, David Geffen, J. Paul Getty, Dizzy Gillespie, Horace Greeley, Tom Hanks, William Hanna, Anne Hathaway, Lillian Hochberg, Dustin Hoffman, Don Imus, Burl Ives, Jane Jacobs, Peter Jennings, Kirk Kerkorian, B.B. King, Ray Kroc, Stan Lee, Doris Lessing, Rush Limbaugh, Barbara Lynch, Steve Madden, Dave Murdoch, Bill Murray, Jack Nelson, David Ogilvy, Jacqueline Kennedy Onassis, George Orwell, Joel Osteen, Sean Parker, Sidney Poitier, Sydney Pollack, Ron Popell, Wolfgang Puck, Dennis Quaid, Rachel Ray, Trent Rezner, Julia Roberts, John D. Rockefeller, Sr., Will Rogers, Karl Rove, William Safire, Vidal Sassoon, and Steven Spielberg, who began his college career at—of all places—Cal State Long Beach.

After being rejected by the USC School of Theater, Film, and Television three times, Spielberg dropped out to work as an unpaid intern in the editing department of Universal Studios. Many years later, after it became clear that he did, in fact, have a gift for filmmaking, USC gave him an honorary degree and made him a trustee. But Spielberg, the child of Orthodox Jews—not unlike Elijah—wanted to set an example for his kids by actually earning his B.A. So, 35 years after beginning his freshman studies, he returned to Cal State Long Beach, completed his remaining course work in Film Production & Electronic Arts, and crossed the same stage where Graham will appear with his classmates later this year.

All of the people listed above became rich beyond their wildest dreams by merely following them. But success pays off in other equally rewarding ways. Just imagine the story of *The King's Speech* without Lionel Logue, a man with no degrees but a talent for acting, a heart for suffering, and a fearless creative spirit that enabled him to help in a way that no credentialed man could—not the clergy, or the doctors, or the new-fangled specialists in speech pathology—just one man who believed in what he could do and brought it to the table, empowering a king to inspire the world, not only in his own time, but still, today, over 60 years later, proving once again that the road less travelled is not quite as risky as we so often portray it. In fact, it just may be the only road that leads us anywhere worth being.

Chapter 8

"Then Elijah said to the prophets of Baal, 'Choose for yourselves one bull and prepare it first, for you are many; then call on the name of your god, but put no fire to it.' So they took the bull that was given them, prepared it, and called on the name of Baal from morning until noon, crying, 'O Baal, answer us!' But there was no voice and no answer." (1 Kings 18: 25-26)

We are a nation held hostage by false gods. We worship money and power, entertainment and gadgets, fashion and fitness, food and booze. We worship our own uniqueness and the clear superiority of our kids. We worship the flag and the right to burn it. We worship the true God in false ways and give our hearts to gods who have no interest in us. When I picture these prophets of Baal crying out for help, I see them in the center of a Best Buy store, their arms raised to a wall of dazzling flat screen TVs that boom and beckon like Oz but only take, take, take—our time, our money, our attention away from the very real needs that might actually be our salvation, our deep joy to meet.

I am as guilty of this as the next American Idol fan. Night after night I chide myself for the sloth of staring at that screen watching shows that add not one thing to my life but mild entertainment. I can't help it. By 8:00 p.m. I'm too tired to be productive, to start something new, to save the world. I set the alarm for 5:00 a.m. and choke back the dread of the early morning hour, imagine some later life when I will be disciplined even in these waning hours, eschewing the TV to sit in an armchair reading important works (will I be smoking a pipe?), or standing behind a counter in a soup kitchen downtown serving food to people whose lives I keep a safe distance from.

Remy has a heart for the homeless. Thanks to her, we now drive around with bottles of water and boxes of granola bars and hand them out on street corners as we travel our daily routes. It's a start. Last year at Christmas I told the kids what I wanted was for them to plan an outing over the holidays that involved us all doing a service project together: Graham looked into a few things, Remy was excited about the idea. But nothing materialized. Why should it? This was the sort of thing I should have done, that Lon and I should have initiated more of, but it is so easy to eat our turkey and stuffing all snug in our beds watching movies we've seen a thousand times, entertaining ourselves to death, basking in our warm, lazy stupors, counting our blessings.

"Oh TV, TV, save us," we cry out each night. And although it shows up right on schedule, it can never answer our prayers.

Over the years many expectant parents have asked me for my advice about raising kids. I always say the same thing. Make sure they're comfortable with silence. Don't turn the TV on first thing in the morning; don't let them turn it on first thing when they come home. Let them know what it feels like to be alone in a room with no distractions, just the sound of their own breath, their own thoughts. I have offered this advice to dozens of couples and almost all of them have responded with a blank stare and a pinched smile.

It's no wonder. Nearly 90% of American households turn the television on first thing when they wake up. Normal in America is now life with a soundtrack of voices and music all playing too loudly, all designed to persuade and amuse, to rile and incense. Without it, we tend to grow restless, twitchy. We reach for our laptops, our smart phones, our ear buds. Our children have disappeared into a conch shell of pre-selected music—only exactly what they want to hear 24 hours a day—pirated from the internet and funneled incessantly into their thirsty, adolescent minds. Anything to drown out the terrible, alien silence that threatens to remind us of—what? What am I missing? What have I done?

"O Baal, save us!!" we cry. And the silence is deafening.

So the god of Baal had a day to make fire. There was a hard stop deadline and one acceptable outcome. Each hour, as his 450 overly-dramatic prophets cried out, the pressure grew. Elijah waited patiently, bemused, as the crowd stirred and fretted. What would become of them if the god they'd chosen to believe in did not come through? If the altar they'd taught their kids to bow down before was revealed as a sham?

So it is with the narrow window of time in which our children are expected to make fire of their lives by producing a winning transcript. Child development specialists of every ilk will tell you that developmental stages have variation, that one thing must build upon the next, and that, although some patterns are predictable, each child is unique. And yet we've created a system in which they are being asked to have a swab taken of their academic DNA during a specific 24-month window, a window in which they are hard-wired to be more concerned about who their real friends are, and what deep inside of them might carry them through to adulthood, and if anyone will ever love them truly, madly, deeply. Like picture day when you have a great big cold sore—and no, you can't reschedule—this is the moment, this blink of their long, potential-filled lives, when we take a quick scan and stamp them like boxes of meat; Prime. Choice. Great on the Grill.

The California High School Proficiency Exam was in nine days. Remy had studied ardently, keeping up with her regular coursework, adding test prep review to her day, continuing her skating each morning. She thrived on clear, attainable goals, and lots of them. Still the fact remained, her new life was not in our control. Despite her enthusiasm and my sense of divine guidance, it was entirely possible that she would panic, or blank out, or get a string of questions that weren't as much in her zone as other questions might have been—miss the whole thing by a point. The next test was not until March with results posted in late April, nearly the end of her junior year, too late to do much good.

I began to consider what I'd do if she didn't pass. If those cold, hard numbers which dictate a life didn't fall our way. Would I pull her anyway? Would I break the law and let her study at home till the next test? Is it even legal for someone to tell me what I can do with my 16-year old child? Each day at Venice High had become more frustrating, the budget cuts in California pressing in on the kids in ways that few could possibly thrive under. One of her classes was in a trailer with 63 kids—not a single one of them white but her. Thankfully, the teacher, Mr. Sandoval, inspired her more than any teacher she'd ever had.

On Monday, five days before the test, Remy woke up with the kind of head cold that forces synapses to slog through oatmeal to form even perfunctory thoughts. In the car on the way to school I asked her questions she knew the day before—*and an allegory is?*—and got a blank stare. By that afternoon she no longer looked like someone who could pull this off. Her teachers, overwhelmed by their growing class sizes, were doubling up on time-consuming, easy-to-grade worksheets. I looked over Remy's day planner and knew something had to give.

"Finish your snack," I said. "Then we're going to have you take a reading comprehension practice test."

"But I've got to do my real homework first. She gave out two more worksheets in English. There's so much type on them I can't even read it." Budget cuts had been forcing teachers to cram four pages of information onto one two-sided sheet in a size-8 font. "I tried to read them the whole class. I still have no idea what I'm even supposed to do."

I could see the fear rising up. Reading comprehension was the greatest bugaboo, the area in which she would undo herself if it came to that. "We'll figure that out later," I said. "Right now you're going to take another practice test."

"No," she protested weakly.

"Just the reading part."

"I can't."

"You have to. Right now."

Ever since we'd decided to go down this path, there was an unspoken reprieve from mother/daughter disagreements: Remy knew that whatever I said was only to help her get what she wanted. She filled up her water bottle and sat down at the table, finishing the test in 40 minutes, 54 questions of fiction and non-fiction passages, practical and technical reading analysis, synonyms and vocabulary in context. I tallied the score in private, no less fearful than she was. When I was done, I knocked on her bedroom door. Entered gently.

"This is a really hard week for you. You're tired, you're sick, you already had a long day at school and you are feeling overwhelmed about all the hours of homework you have left. This is the worst possible time for you to perform well on a test." Her eyes tightened, bracing for the news. "And you passed, no problem," I smiled.

She shot her arms up in the air and shouted, "YES!"

This was the experience I wanted her to own. Even if she woke up Saturday morning with a fever and a head full of GACK, she had it in her to get the job done.

"Remember that," I told her, and she nodded calmly, confidently, and with a slight uptick in energy to approach the stack of work that still remained.

Time is a character in every story and this one is no exception. The nearer we got to the exam date, the harder it was to enforce the daily requirements of her high school workload. Each night I lowered the standard a little bit more, so that she was no longer really aspiring to her best possible showing in her junior year, but merely ensuring that she didn't dig herself into a such a big hole that if things went horribly wrong and she had to finish out the year at Venice High, she'd be able to rally. I took my cues from the bumper sticker wisdom of Albert Einstein: "You can't simultaneously prevent and prepare for war."

The PSATs were being given at Venice on Wednesday of that week. Nearly all of the students in her classes would be taking them; Remy would not. I decided the time would be better spent taking a full CHSPE practice test in an unfamiliar setting. I let her sleep in, skate an hour, then dropped her off at a public library two towns over. She needed to be in a strange place, to figure out where the clock was and how to keep track of it, how to overlook the glances of strangers and stay in the zone. I told her I'd be back in 3 ½ hours.

Two and half hours later, Remy texted me. Done! With a smiling emoticon. I was more suspicious than encouraged. Her biggest challenge had always been moving too slowly through tests, not being able to finish, then getting distracted by all the kids who were done early. "Did you double check everything?" I asked.

"Yep. I went really slowly. I'm good."

I was not wholly convinced until I read her practice essay. The question had been about lowering the drinking age to 18 and whether or not she thought that was a good idea. It was the best thing she'd ever written, not just creatively, or in her use of grammar—which had always been strong—but in her absolute adherence to the strict rules of essay writing: thesis statement and support paragraphs and refuting of the opposition. On a scale of 1-5, which this paper would be graded on, it would likely earn the top points. But what I'll remember about this paper forever was the basis in fact she used as her primary argument for why the drinking age should not be lowered: "At the age of 18, the brain is not fully developed. It does not reach maturity until the age of 21."

Graham would be 21 in ten days. Who he was as a junior in high school and who he is now—not only in life but on paper—is the difference between a boy and a man, a young man left to his own devices to grow and strive as he felt pulled. I knew him to be a boy of good character, kind, wise, smart, circumspect, but the way those qualities were playing out in his life, and the way he'd built on all that he'd learned from his baseball years—the drive, the focus, the work ethic, the people skills—to create startling yet familiar possibilities, took my breath away. Looking at his cumulative file at 17, no stranger would have ever detected this level of excellence in him.

After her practice test, I drove Remy over to University High School where her real test would be given on Saturday. She liked to be familiar with a setting beforehand. We drove around the campus, and I told her it was a lucky place for our family: I had taken the SATs there 30 years before, could still remember the feeling of stepping out of my mom's car and walking up to the big, brick building with my #2 pencils in hand. It was also the place where Graham had pitched a no-hitter in his junior year. "And now it's the place where you'll pass your CHSPE," I said, and regretted, instantly my presumption. The God I knew could bless her life with a pass or a fail and it was not my place to say what He had in mind.

That night was the third meeting of our Peacemaker study at church. I was leading one of the groups with my friend, Rachel (the Rachel who helped find our tenant, not Rachel the next-door neighbor). Twenty people joined in the sanctuary to watch a short video before breaking off into two smaller groups to discuss the material.

The principles of the Peacemaker program are deceptively simple and can be used by anyone, of any faith, or none. My friend and prayer partner, Sarah, had pointed out to me that they were remarkably similar to Stephen Covey's principles for effective people, only he would replace the first step, Glorify God, with the more secular idea of Win-Win. The program begins with a working definition of conflict: "A difference in opinion or purpose that frustrates someone's goals or expectations." It seems obvious, but unlike how it feels to be in conflict in real life, the definition was not personal or emotional, just matter of fact. Two people, two factions, with differing goals based on differing purposes, played out in the same space.

Tonight's video was on the second step— **"Taking the log out of your own eye"**—which is based on Matthew 7:3-5. The lecture included this explanation: the reason we find it so easy to see the speck in our neighbor's eyes and not the logs in our own is that we have created false idols for ourselves. And these false idols—which might include control or efficiency or accomplishment or material comfort—lead us down a slippery slope so that what at first we only desire, soon we demand. Then we judge others who don't see it as we do. Then we punish them for getting in our way. This was no study for the happily deluded. Well, actually it was, but it was unlikely they'd attend.

After the video, I led the six ladies in our group into the small den that was used on Sundays as a cry room. There, in the darkened hallway outside our door appeared a small African-American woman neatly dressed in contemporary tribal garb. "I'm looking for the principal," she said in the native tones of a distant land.

"He's not here right now," I said. "Would you like me to call him for you?"

Before the woman could answer, Rachel appeared behind her. "This is the mother of one of our new confirmands," she said to me, pointedly. "She's here to pick her up."

Rachel and I had both been at the church since 6:30. The Vicar, along with the 7 & 8th grade teacher, had sent the last of the confirmation students home, as scheduled, at 6:00 p.m. There were no children left. Rachel and Sarah and I circled round the African mother and tried to radiate grace and calm as the Vicar pulled out his cell phone and began working through the list of young families who'd left there with their kids an hour before.

"I'm sure she went home with a friend," I said, based on nothing more than it being a benign explanation. I scrambled to think of a classmate whose parents I might know well enough to have their number in my phone, but couldn't. For a dozen years I had been so intimately involved with the school that by October of any given year, I could tell you every single student's name. This new disconnect, born of my own kids moving on, made me feel impotent.

The members of the Peacemaker groups were beginning to peek out, curious, concerned. A parish hall full of speculating adults wouldn't help anyone. Rachel, who is an Elder in our church, told me to get our group started, told Sarah to take the other group. I returned to the cry room and sat in the empty chair. "Let's pray."

"Gracious and heavenly Father, we ask your blessing on this young girl and her mother whose heart is sick with worry. We do not know in this moment where she is but trust in your love and care for her. Please keep her safe and lead us to the information we need for this situation to be resolved quickly and well. And please still our fearful hearts as we attempt to concentrate on your Word through this study, so that each of our lives may give glory to you, even in times of uncertainty. Bless the women in this room, who help me to understand myself and your Gospel a little bit more clearly each week. Let our hearts be open tonight to the truth you have prepared for each one of us. Amen."

We opened our Peacemaker booklets and began to discuss the challenges of taking the logs out of our own eyes, confessing how much we tend to be short-tempered with our loved ones, how our need to control situations leads us to behave in ways we're not proud of. We tried to understand the difference between the conflict we experience in our personal lives and the conflict we may experience in the workplace: most of the women in the room were smart and successful and worked in supervisory roles. Each of us had struggled with trying to enforce high standards at work only to be met with resistance by less motivated or underskilled employees. We wrestled with how behavior is impacted by financial expectations and how the truth of the bottom line was often at odds with the biblical truth of loving one's neighbor.

There was a panel of glass between the cry room and the darkened sanctuary. Through the glass I could see and hear Vicar pacing back and forth making calls to parents he'd just met. He'd only been with us four months. In the spring he was still in seminary, spending his evenings juggling his studies with the needs of his wife and two young children. Then, pastoral care was purely theoretical. Now, there was a missing child on his watch.

I returned my attention to the women in the room and began to cry. I said that I feared that the demanding schedule I'd put our family on to support Remy's love of skating had become a false idol that was now chipping away not only at her but at the fabric of our lives. Even though I believed deeply in letting her pursue her passion, the reality of it, the morning after morning after morning had worn thin. Lon and I had, at one point, taken turns, but now that he was working every day an hour away, this was mine to carry. Many nights we'd only see each other for an hour and then for little more than a shared moment of TV. Mornings were a blur, rising in the dark, whispering hurriedly, struggling to remember books and snacks and skates and hurrying, always hurrying, eyes still bleary, the schedule driving everything. And I had allowed it to happen.

Suddenly, there was a guttural wail from the parish hall, the sort of noise that is only brought forth from a mother's chest, heaving and sobbing as if a child had just fallen into an abyss. The cry room fell silent. We stared at each other wide-eyed, frozen, our hearts a held-breath prayer as we waited for God's very real presence to calm the pained cries. We dropped our booklets and took each other's hands. The primordial voice shifted. Now there was anger, the mother shouting, enraged, her accent making the fury seem as if it had come straight from the bloody belly of

Creation. I thought of Vicar and Rachel standing there, absorbing the rage as she blamed the church for some awful unknown thing that had happened to her daughter—what was it? What had happened? I closed my eyes and I tilted my head one degree to the right and there it was. I could hear it now, the distinct hint of relief in that rage. The universal sound of a mother screaming at a child for scaring the living daylights out of her.

"Excuse me," I said again and ran out.

In the parish hall, alone at a table sat a confused looking black girl, no more than twelve. Rachel led the mother down the hall to the room where I would later discover the daughter had been all along, had simply stayed there after her group had broken up, alone in a little loft space in the dark—whether studying or praying or napping or trying to get attention, we'll never know—but there all along, in the room in the house of God. Vicar sighed gratefully and gave me a thumbs-up as he continued with his phone calls, circling back to each worried parent.

The ladies in my group were relieved and eager now to return to our discussion about false idols and how they blind us. A mother of three who had recently sent her youngest off to college began to share her concerns. She was distressed because her son had called her just that day to report his first collegiate midterm grade. A 13/15. While the mother had been thrilled, her son was disappointed. "I had studied really hard," he had told her. "I should have gotten a perfect score." She hung her head in a way I'd never seen before: she was a bright, cheerful soul, a pre-school teacher, a deeply faithful woman. "I'm worried I did this to him. Made him think he had to be perfect. Everything we've done to get him into a good school. All the tests, all the studying. We just talked about grades so much."

Up until that moment I imagined that all the parents who pushed too hard to reach the goal were ignorant of the possible damage; we were not. We had just decided that the risk was too great not to play the game. But the game had consequences. Mark C. Davis, Chairman of the department of religion—not business or engineering—at Columbia University shared this observation about one of his recent classes:

"The students were working hard and performing well but there was no energy in our discussions and no passion in the students. They were hesitant to express their ideas and often seemed to be going through the motions. I tried to encourage them to be more venturesome with tactics I had used successfully in the past but nothing worked. One day I asked them what was or, perhaps better, was not going on. Why were they so cautious and where was their enthusiasm for learning? They seemed relieved to talk about it and their response surprised me. Since pre-kindergarten, they explained, they had been programmed to perform well so they could get to the next level. They had been taught the downside of risk and encouraged to play it safe. What mattered most was getting into a good elementary school, middle school and high school so that they would finally be admitted to a top college. Having succeeded beyond their parents' wildest expectations, they did not know why they were in college and had no idea what to do after graduation."

There were a handful of jobs—teacher, counselor, naturalist—that I could imagine Remy wanting to do one day that would require a degree. But none of them would require that she got into a top college straight out of high school. And the more likely path, one involving her gift for any number of art forms, would not require a degree at all. Artists are by nature self-taught.

When Remy was seven years old I found her late one summer evening at the kitchen table. She had a pad and a flashlight and a ruler and a pencil.

"What are you doing?" I asked.

"I'm seeing how to make the shadows from the pencil shorter or longer. See, if I move the flashlight, it changes."

Normally I am a stickler for bedtimes, but I knew that all the tools she'd need to grow into herself had been planted for her in that moment. "Take your time," I said. "Take your time."

Time, I knew, is the one thing that all artists need most.

With the sound of a mother's haunted cries still ringing in my ears, I came home and turned on the TV. It was the day the Chilean miners were rescued. I had not followed the story closely, as many had, but now stared transfixed as the miners were raised up, hugging, cheering, looking remarkably healthy and well. For 69 days they had been trapped in Hell. Many had entered the half-mile-deep tomb as men of faith: all arose that way. In a world starved for inspiration, it came in the form of 33 dirt-smeared laborers who learned how to survive as a team, a community—a Body—who downplayed each other's weaknesses and maximized each other's strengths and, in doing so, showed the world, even for an instant, how to do the same. There were no false idols in that hole.

Chapter 9

No one knows how old Elijah was when he arrived at Ahab's palace to prophesy the end of the rain. The days that followed—at the Wadi Cherith and with the widow and all the way up to this, the showdown at Mount Carmel—numbered well over a thousand. Not long after, he grows weary and is ready to pass the torch. Judging from my own tired bones, I think it's safe to say he was not 20 or even 30 years old but more likely in his 40s when he first entered the biblical narrative, begging the question: what had he been doing all those years before that? As a prophet, he wouldn't have had any other job. Jewish law at the time dictated that all prophets of the LORD were to be fed and given basic support so they could serve the people in word and truth. But in the years leading up to the drought, the people were growing increasingly distant from the God of Abraham and Isaac and Jacob. It would have fallen upon Elijah to warn them that they were going astray. This was likely the primary activity of his early adult life: shouting out admonishments from this very mountaintop, pounding on Ahab and Jezebel's door in the wee hours, exhorting high-flying Samarians who, no doubt, blew clouds of sweet smoke in Elijah's importunate face and shouted "Prig!"

Now, after living with the effects of the long, hard drought—the one Elijah had proclaimed—the people find themselves more inclined to listen. All morning long they had watched their prophets "limp about the altar" in vain. Unable to stand idly by, Elijah suddenly takes on the role of cheerleader, revealing a heretofore unseen gift for snarkiness:

"Cry aloud! Surely he is a god: either he is meditating, or he has wandered away, or he is on a journey, or perhaps he is asleep and must be awakened."

In ancient days the term "wandered away" was a euphemism for going to the bathroom. "Cry out!" Elijah taunts them, and the prophets of the false gods begin...

"...slashing themselves with swords and lances as the blood gushed out over them. As midday passed, they raved on until the time of the oblation (dusk), but there was no voice, no answer, and no response." (1 Kings 18:27-29)

There is nothing new under the sun. The slashing of bodies, once the realm of religious zealots, is now a popular emotional outlet for American teens. Cutting—the act of breaking the skin without intent to cause death—is on the rise not only in teenaged girls, but in our boys, as well. Some say it's a cry for help, others a way of being outrageous. All agree that it is evidence that teens, who've been tormented souls since the dawn of time, are finding it now more unbearable than ever. Cutting allows them to transfer their mental pain to a physical form, as the adrenalin rushes in to numb the inflammation at the site. Journalist Nicci Gerrard summed it up this way: "They're not stupid or mad, but maybe they are trying to tell us something about their inner lives and can't find the words. So they unscrew the blade of their pencil sharpener and draw it over their skin. Blood flows. 'Look at me', they're saying. 'Look how I hurt. Look.' And we should look."

In her freshman year at Venice High, Remy got her first real exposure to how most teens talk nowadays. The F-bomb was dropped every other word and sex was discussed like sport. She struggled to keep her peace of mind as all around her kids shouted and tussled and barbed. Drugs were passed in the aisles. Backpacks reeked of pot. Boys pressed girls up against lockers in ways that made passersby feel they were intruding.

The quality of student was much higher in the magnet classes, but we had opted out of the magnet for Remy because it required an additional six courses in languages and global social studies, preventing students from taking art or drama until senior year. I had placed her in the New Media Academy and prayed it would be a good fit. It wasn't. Nearly ¾ of the 9th grade class of New Media students would end up having to repeat the grade. An English teacher, Dennis Danzinger, noticed Remy's giftedness in writing the first day of school and urged the counselors to put her in his Honors class. Their first big assignment was to create a children's book with pictures and text. Remy spent a good 50 hours on it. On the day it was due, she brought it in proudly, encased in a protective gallon-sized Ziploc bag. There was only one other student in the class who had done the assignment; his, a one-page, hand-written sheet with some Post-it note stick figures slapped on at the last minute.

"It'll get better," we promised. The bad students, we calculated, would not be able to move on to 10th grade, or would drop out all together. "Hang in there," we told her. As if to protect herself, she started bringing her Bible to school for free reading. She walked around with it open, her head bowed in the text—this, from the girl who hated to read. "I'm going to read the whole Bible straight through," she told me. "But I'm not going to take a whole year like you did. I'm going to get it done before school's out." And she did.

In her sophomore year, she had packets of KY jelly left on her books and fielded daily innuendos, many of which went straight over her head. She was force searched in a random classroom drug raid, and worried that her bottle of Purell might somehow get her in trouble. She was asked to identify pills exchanged in a drug deal that took place right under her nose in the back of her World History class. She was tormented by a Spanish teacher who hated white kids and took delight in humiliating them. Despite all the challenges, she would tell me that it was making her strong; so strong that there was nothing she couldn't handle, no challenge, no obstacle, no adversity. She had some tremendous teachers who cared for her and watched out for her and advised her—Mr. Smith, Ms. Sabbah, The Alcantars, Ms. Roche-Blair, Ms. Debenning, Ms. Ruiz—all who gave me enough reassurance to feel that her experience was more good than bad.

It was during these years that she developed a passion for uplifting the unfortunate, seeking particularly to mentor struggling minority kids. Daily she'd ask to drive through The Projects, to see, to understand. It was all I could do to stop her from jumping out of the car and knocking on doors with offers of help. What sort of help she planned to provide for them at this point was ill-defined, but her heroes were Erin Gruwell, the teacher from *Freedom Writers*, and Leigh Anne Tuohy, the mom from *The Blind Side*.

"You have a little more to learn yourself," I'd tell her.

"Maybe," she said. "But I'm already helping people now."

While other pony-tailed blonde girls were sabotaging each other's dreams and doing tequila shooters and sneaking out of windows while their moms scoured the internet for college application tips, Remy would tell me—with the sort of excitement usually reserved for invitations to the prom—that her friend whose dad was in prison and whose mom had od'ed, had gotten a C+ on his test! That she had had a nice lunch with a new student whose mother had died the month before. He was living with his grandma because his father had rejected him; Remy suspected it was because he was gay. In the spring of her sophomore year, she had gotten a text from a girl she'd met once, for three hours, at an audition for the spring musical. The girl had just gotten out of the hospital where she had been taken after a suicide attempt. Remy didn't even recognize the name when it came through her screen but the girl told her she thought Remy might be the only person who could help her feel better. Remy talked with her for over an hour, about the gifts God had given her for acting, about how that joy was her way to find a reason to live again. At night, on Facebook, she would chat with guys with no goals and no future, encouraging them to stop partying and start doing their homework in a tone that was both self-effacing and funny and utterly serious. "I'm so proud of you for not smoking any pot all last week. If you need any other ideas for drug-free fun, just let me know!!!"

It is one of the messages of the Cross that we are to meet our humanity through suffering, that we will be healed through the process of helping others heal, that God will enter that crucible with us. Without the experience of Venice High, the Gospel would be nothing but theory. With it, Remy had taken full possession of the power of Christ.

The CHSPE was two days away. I kept Remy out of school again. The only goal now was to keep her rested and healthy until the test. We slept in and skated later in the morning. All her efforts were more productive; mine too. I could feel the ball of fuzzy tension in my head disappearing. It was a beautiful fall morning, the air warm and bright. I walked from a local coffee shop back to the rink and felt as if the weight of the day, of all our days, had been lifted. Driving home it was Remy who spoke first.

"So I know that the odds are I'll pass this test. I mean, like 99% chance." It was the first time I'd even heard her acknowledge even the tiniest possibility of failure: her approach to any goal was absolute success—there was to be no talk of anything less. Fortunately, she was fairly even-keeled in accepting a range of outcomes after the fact.

"You've passed every practice test you've taken, that's for sure."

"But, I mean, if I don't, well, couldn't I just be homeschooled until the next test?" There was no begging in her voice. She was calm, practical, logical.

Although I hadn't dared to speak of it, the idea had been on my mind with increasing frequency. With each day I became more convinced that despite all the stress and the effort, everything she was doing in high school was more about survival than learning. Even the five weeks we'd need to wait for the test results were starting to feel like more than I could rally for.

"Maybe," I said.

I could feel Remy hold herself stock still, as if we were playing a game of Freeze Tag; one false move and she feared she might nudge the answer in the wrong direction.

We pulled in the driveway and I went straight to my laptop to begin researching the laws about homeschooling. California, it turns out, is one of the few states that requires a child to be in school full-time till the age of 18. If she were to simply stop going, she would be truant and we would be legally responsible. I laughed to think that with all the LAUSD budget cuts there would somehow be money to send someone to my house to check up on us. But I preferred to exercise creativity and independence within the limits of the law. Reading further, I discovered I could establish a private school in my home. All that was required was that I took attendance every day and could show work

135

in progress if asked. I already had syllabi forming in my head.

I clicked on the link that explained the process for becoming an official, legally-recognized private school. There was a two-week period of registration each year. No registration was allowed before or after that two-week window. No exceptions. As it happened, the registration time was October 1-15. It was the 14th. The option would be off the table in 24 hours. Remy and I prayed and then we called Lon.

This, for me, was the hardest step. I knew I would not move forward without Lon's blessing. I had learned from experience that despite me taking my cues from above, my life was designed as a partnership and we were all better off when Lon and I worked in tandem. I spat out the details quickly and held my breath. In his own minimalist fashion, Lon replied with a laugh. "Sounds like we lucked out on the timing."

By 2:30 p.m., I had filed paperwork online with the state, officially opening the Davis Academy. I then called Venice High and told them Remy would be withdrawing. The lady in the attendance office said to bring in a letter from her new school for the file. I opened up an InDesign document and created our new letterhead: *Davis Academy, Excellence in Individualized Learning*, and jotted off a note from me, the official Headmaster. Just like that, the CHSPE test no longer mattered. If she passed, she would work at home till the spring semester started at Santa Monica College. If she didn't, she would work at home a few months longer. In the end, it wouldn't make a bit of difference. We had prayed and we had listened and we had obeyed. Sometimes change comes just by waiting it out. Other times, it takes violent action.

If there were a soundtrack to the showdown at Mt. Carmel it would be *Carmina Burana*. Good vs evil, dramatic slashing and wailing, the whole nation holding its breath, and the real fireworks haven't even begun. We join Elijah now, ready for his close-up:

"Then Elijah said to all the people, 'Come closer to me;' and all the people came closer to him."

"First he repaired the altar of the LORD that had been thrown down; Elijah took twelve stones, according to the number of the tribes of the sons of Jacob, to whom the word of the LORD came, saying, 'Israel shall be your name'; with the stones he built an altar in the name of the LORD."

"Then he made a trench around the altar, large enough to contain two measures of seed. Next he put the wood in order, cut the bull in pieces, and laid it on the wood. He said, 'Fill four jars with water and pour it on the burnt offering and on the wood.'"

"Then he said, 'Do it a second time'; and they did it a second time. Again he said, 'Do it a third time': and they did it a third time, so that the water ran all around the altar, and filled the trench also with water."
(1 Kings 18: 30-35)

Skepticism is as old as time. Elijah knew that there would be people who would claim that the fire he was about to produce was some sort of spontaneous combustion—just as they would later say that Moses' parting of the Red Sea was merely low tide, or that the stories of loaves and fishes were exaggerated potlucks, and of course, that someone simply rolled the stone away so Jesus could slip out of the tomb unnoticed. Elijah made sure that the altar and the bull and every inch of space in even moderate proximity was soaked through. There would be no other explanation.

"At the time of the offering of the oblation, the prophet Elijah came near and said, 'O LORD, God of Abraham, Isaac, and Israel, let it be known this day that you are God in Israel, that I am your servant, and that I have done all these things at your bidding.'"

"Answer me, O LORD, answer me, so that this people may know that you, O LORD, are God, and that you have turned their hearts back.'" (1 Kings 18:36-37)

Elijah did not limp or beg or tear his clothes, bleed or wail or engage in theatrics. Rather, when it came time to pray he asked *sotto voce* for the LORD to make His presence real. What the people witnessed that day would appear effortless, a man asking for a miracle and knowing it would come.

"Then the fire of the LORD fell and consumed the burnt offering, the wood, the stones, and the dust, and even licked up the water that was in the trench.

When all the people saw it, they fell on their faces and said, 'The LORD indeed is God.'" (1 Kings 18:38-39)

Elijah had them right where God wanted them. Humble, contrite, ready to repent. How would he harness that power for good? Perhaps a confession service, a group prayer, a sung recitation of the *Shema Yisrael*? Whatever Elijah said, they would do, for surely he spoke at the bidding of the LORD. The people looked up from the ground, eyes opened anew and now raised, and awaited Elijah's next word:

"Elijah said to them, 'Seize the prophets of Baal; do not let one of them escape.' Then they seized them; and Elijah brought them down to the Wadi Kishon, and killed them there." (1 Kings 18:40)

Four hundred and fifty prophets of Baal. Four hundred prophets of Asherah. All put to death if not by Elijah's own hand, then under his supervision. Why? Where is the love? Where is the forgiveness? How can this act of punitive rage ever be reconciled to a loving, merciful God? It would be several hundred years before Christ would come and speak about the folly of "putting new wine in old wine skins," but a contemporary of Elijah's, the prophet Isaiah, offers some insight:

"A voice cries out: in the wilderness, prepare the way of the LORD, make straight in the desert a highway for our God." (Isaiah 40:3)

A straight path to God is not one littered with distractions, dissuasions, temptations, and all matter of underminers. God had won the battle. He had deigned to prove himself. He did not plan to do it again the next week, when the people's minds had grown flabby and the whispers of the false prophets had begun to make them question what they had seen with their own eyes. Although the violence seems, to modern, pacifist ears, both shocking and cold-hearted, the reaction is not unlike us finding our seven-year olds watching videos of half-naked ladies singing songs about *brushing their teeth with a bottle of Jack* and deciding to wield parental protection blocks on the whole cable package. With too much competing noise, God can never get a word in edgewise. And so, at Mt. Carmel, the LORD instructed Elijah to do what any good parent would do to protect her kids, so easily distracted, so easily fallen prey. He took the enemy out. We may not like his methods, but we cannot fail to admire his devotion.

There is a term in sound design called "cross fading." I remember learning it the first time I produced a radio commercial. I was 18 and thought that the dark rooms with the sound booths and the buttons and the actors who came and went and made my words come to life were like working in a dream. On those big engineering boards there are dozens of sliding controls that make things louder and softer, brighter or duller. When you simultaneously lower one level while raising another so that there is an almost imperceptible shift of dominance and focus, this is called cross fading.

Over the last 40 years, the practice of incorporating religion into our children's daily life has become a matter for the courts. Christmas, a holiday celebrated, according to a

2000 Reuters study, by 96% of Americans—including over 80% of non-Christians—has become a hotbed for conflict. Leading civil rights attorneys have even created The Twelve Rules of Christmas® to help well-meaning souls navigate the civic mess created out of our desire to be considerate of those of other faiths, no faith, or even those who like the idea of Christmas but don't want to be reminded about the Jesus part. Here are three examples:

- Public schools may teach students about the Christmas holiday, including its religious significance, so long as it is taught objectively for secular purposes such as its historical or cultural importance, and not for the purpose of promoting Christianity.

- Public schools may include Christmas music, including those with religious themes, in their choral programs if the songs are included for a secular purpose such as their musical quality or cultural value or if the songs are part of an overall performance including other holiday songs relating to Chanukah, Kwanzaa, or other similar holidays.

- Public schools may not require students to sing Christmas songs whose messages conflict with the students' own religious or nonreligious beliefs.

As the soundtrack of God has been decreased by

man, another has risen up. The song of Better Get Mine Now cause there's not going to be anything coming later. This is the Song that has driven capitalism amok and forced the pressures all the way down to the grade school level where *Silent Night* has been supplanted by innocuous tunes about snowmen and winter wonderlands; Muzak in the place of mystery, sugar cookies in lieu of Eternal Love so as never to offend.

A few curious notes, though, have managed to break through our secular deep freeze—notably, a resurgence in the art of Gregorian chant, the Psalm-based sung-prayers of monks through the ages. Concert series at major universities now routinely include chant choirs in their repertoires, always to sell-out crowds. Hildegard of Bingen, a medieval nun who was not only a writer of chants but a mystic, a botanist, a poet, and a painter of illuminated manuscripts, has become something of a rising star in circles of high culture. Even Lon has been known to download the occasional esoteric chant collection on iTunes.

One thread of this sacred movement was begun during World War II, high on a hill in the countryside of Taize, France. There, a man named Brother Roger bought a small house with some outlying buildings so he could offer hospitality to refugees. "There was no running water....Food was simple, mainly soups made from corn flour bought cheaply at the nearby mill. Out of discretion towards those he was sheltering, Brother Roger prayed alone; he often went to sing far from the house, in the woods, so that none of the refugees, Jews or agnostics, would feel ill at ease."

His sister helped him care for their visitors and, at the end of the war, they began to take in the orphans. Gradually, other young men felt called to help serve along side him and within a few years, they had formed a monastic community, taking vows of celibacy and simplicity. They would not be beholden to any denomination, but only to the purest distillation of Christ's truth. From that foundation of community, Brother Roger and his monks began to write simple, resonant song refrains that captured the longing for a connection with God in a way that spoke to people all over the world. And so the people came— from Chile and New Zealand, China and Bangladesh, from all across Europe and the Americas. The monks added new buildings, expanded the chapel, began to record their songs in all the languages of the world.

"Right at the depth of the human condition, lies the longing for a presence, the silent desire for a communion. Let us never forget that this simple desire for God is already the beginning of faith." Brother Alois, Taize

Over the last 70 years, Taize has become a true global village, with a primary mission of reaching out to the world's young people in their most critical coming-of-age years, 17-29. Over 30,000 young seekers and believers make pilgrimages there each year, to eat and sleep and pray in community, and to sing together under a massive, white, candlelit tent these simple songs of hope and peace... *"Look to God, do not be afraid, Lift up your voices, the LORD is near, Lift up your voices, the LORD is near."*

A song like this was being sung during an evening service when Brother Roger, at the age of 90, was stabbed to death by a deranged visitor. In celebration of the five-year anniversary of his death, the community has been disseminating video excerpts from his talks to people all over the world. I wish I could show it to you, to give you a chance to see the gentleness in his face, but we are left now with only his words. Here, from an excerpt called Wounded Innocence:

"There is in childhood a huge portion of innocence. It can be wounded by unexpected events that no one wished, but the innocence was wounded. And starting from those wounds, every human being, at any age, can react in such a way that he defends himself without realizing it. And sometimes that goes so far that it can often lead to hatred. But every human being, every woman, every man, every child, needs to grasp that if there is violence in the world, they have to begin in themselves to search, to begin to liberate themselves from hatred, from inner violence, and discover the little road, quite simple, of trust of heart, of listening. Not trying to be right, not tiring out others by one's own good reasons. No, listening, with the certainty that the other is inhabited by what he is unaware of."

Our neighbor Tina is a clown. Seriously. It is her gift to bring joy into any room, but on this night the spark looked as if it had been snuffed clear out of her. Her son had just started kindergarten at the neighborhood public school. It was the very same school that the director of *Waiting for Superman* rejected (not easily), choosing to put his own children into private school. I would see them walk there together as a family in the morning, Tina and Tim, Keaton and Adelaide. Keaton is one of the most winning young boys I've ever met: full of life and joy and athleticism and uncanny people skills. It is not uncommon for him to say, "I really like that dress, Heather," or "I had such a good day today; let me tell you about it." Evidently, his kindergarten teacher wasn't seeing things the same way.

"The teacher says he's behind," Tina said as she collapsed on my couch. Her face was so void of light I almost didn't recognize her.

"How could he be behind?" I said. "He's in kindergarten. School just started."

This was the first school year since the *L.A. Times* began publishing the value-added teacher performance statistics, announcing to the world whether or not a teacher was effective. Every measurement creates a new pressure, which inevitably gets shoved down on the kids.

"His printing isn't neat enough, they say."

I tried not to laugh, thinking back on all the years that Graham's papers had come home—year after year after year—with a note at the top NEATNESS PLEASE. Graham focused on the content. Now he just types. Can't say that his handwriting ever got any better.

There is not an age or stage at which the world will not attempt to tell us whether or not we, or our kids, are cutting it. This leads invariably to the trap of fear and shame and on into a cycle of judgment and blame that erupts in the sort of violence that scars children for life. In Taize, they believe that the only way to break the cycle is to learn to trust. Just that. To listen and to trust. Trust in God. Trust in each other. It sounds so simple, doesn't it? But we can't for the life of us bring ourselves to do it.

Chapter 10

Cloud seeding has been around since the early 1940s, but didn't enter the public consciousness until the Beijing Olympics in 2008. That's when the Chinese government's determination to put on the best show ever led them to invest heavily in controlling the weather: no rain on the opening ceremonies, cleansing rain beforehand to clear out the smog, all made possible by rocketing pellets of various chemicals into the sky, forcing the rain clouds to ripen early and clear out. There was a schedule to keep. A timeframe. There was not room for the vagaries of nature.

This seemed to be the last frontier. Until then, we needed God to provide the rain, but science had finally won out; the last fiber of the cord had been broken and we were free. The Chinese put on what was, arguably, the greatest opening ceremonies in Olympic history. Around the globe we marveled at their technological bravado, their artistry, their lock-step teamwork. The Beijing Games were a stroke of PR genius, rebranding the Chinese people in the eyes of most of the world. There was, of course, the issue of the gold-medal winning gymnastics team, which was comprised of members whose government-issued birth certificates seemed to belie their lack of body development. Or teeth.

A year passed before a true investigation was made, not into the women's team of 2008, but all the way back to the team China sent to Sydney in 2000. At least one member was finally proved to have been under age, leading to a disqualification of the entire team. Quietly, and with little fanfare, the "winners" from Team China were asked to return their bronze medals so that they could be redistributed to the fourth place U.S. team. There would be no return trip to Sydney, no podium, no covers on magazines to frame for a lifetime. Just an ordinary spring day a decade after the fact, when FedEx trucks pulled up to the doors of six U.S. girls, now women, fully grown, some with kids of their own, who, one by one, signed for their packages and donned the old bronze medals—the ribbons stained with some other girl's sweat and memories—and tried to convince themselves that justice had been done.

This win-at-all-costs approach that the Chinese have adopted to keep up with—and now overtake—the U.S., has been even more keenly felt in the area of education. In 2010, the Program for International Student Assessment showed China to be outperforming every country in the world in math, science, and reading, casting a dark shadow on America's future. The numbers are not pretty: U.S. students ranked a dismal 31st in math, 23rd in science, and 17th in reading. The only area in which we ranked Number 1 was in self-confidence, an embarrassing symptom of our obsession with giving our kids medals and trophies every time they remember to wipe.

These numbers reveal real problems, but they are not the whole story. Look beyond the headlines and you'll find soul-searching and doubt throughout all of China, as well. "I carry a strong feeling of bitterness," writes Chen Weihua, an editor at the state-run *China Daily*. "The making of superb test-takers comes at a high cost, often killing much of, if not all, the joy of childhood." A vice-principal from a public school in top-ranked Shanghai sees face-to-face what the tests conceal. The students' "creativity is lacking. They suffer very poor health, they are not strong and they get injured easily." Just as America is trying to ratchet up our children's performance, the Chinese government is planning an ambitious overhaul to minimize stress and nurture innovative thinking; just as we can no longer afford a future of wannabee pop stars, China can no longer flourish with a citizenry of automatons.

There is a larger truth at play.

And so it is, that just as the world is quaking over the Chinese gift for test taking, there is, beneath it all, a steady, burgeoning, and little-publicized spiritual revolt. There are now over 100 million Christians in China, people who've found that a life with no purpose other than making money and winning medals and scoring well on tests is not much of a life at all. There are a handful of "sanctioned" churches now, carefully monitored, but the greater movement is the growth of the house church, where each day the new Chinese faithful gather to hear the Gospel and to feel connected for the first time in their lives to something greater than national dominance. Before the Olympic games, the Chinese government swept the house churches clean, forcing them deeper underground. The Games were to be a commercial for China's communist version of capitalism; God, who did not exist, would not have a presence at their coming out party.

But the house churches did not cease to exist. The God of Abraham and Isaac and Jacob, the God who gave His Son so that all might have eternal life, was alive and well from Lhasa to Zhengzhou, and—even as the torch was lit in the Bird's Nest—spreading like wildfire across the communist nation. I see proof of this hunger for Christ in the Chinese people each year when I receive my royalty statements from the release of my first book, a deeply personal and emotional conversion memoir that was translated into only one language.

"Here comes the rain again,
falling on my head like a memory,
falling on my head like a new emotion"
-Eurythmics

Elijah thought that the battle was over. God had won. The false prophets were gone. It was time to let it rain. He said to Ahab, **"Go up, eat and drink: for there is a sound of rushing rain."** There was, in fact, no rain. Not yet. Not that anyone could see. **"Elijah went up to the top of Carmel; there he bowed himself down upon the earth and put his face between his knees."** In yoga, we would call it Child's Pose.

Elijah said to his servant, **"Go up now, look towards the sea."** The servant went up and looked and said, **"There is nothing."** Then Elijah said, **"Go again seven times."** At the seventh time the servant said, **"Look, a little cloud no bigger than a person's hand is rising out of the sea."** (1 Kings 18: 41-44)

This is the very essence of faith. To believe in that which is yet unseen. To keep checking the horizon for it with a child's pure certainty that the promised thing will appear. As we seek to instill in our children all we'd have them be or do or know, imagine if we were to proclaim the sound of the rushing rain of their long lives and trust beyond all reason or proof that God is, as we speak, forming a little cloud no bigger than a person's hand in their hearts. If we were to have only one prayer, what if it were simply this: let it grow.

"In a little while the heavens grew black with clouds and wind: there was a heavy rain." (1 Kings 18:45)

Elijah headed for home, likely thinking of a good meal and a well-earned rest. But Jezebel, who was conveniently absent when her false gods were proved unworthy, had other plans for him. Upon hearing the news about the LORD's showy sovereignty and the bloody corpses of her beloved prophets, she sent Elijah this threat: **"So may the gods do to me, and more also, if I do not make your life like the life of one of them by this time tomorrow."** (1 Kings 19:2)

151

Big whoop, right? I mean, for a man who just summoned the LORD to make fire on cue in front of a cast of thousands, this should seem laughable. The last rants of a dying era of sin and evil. How could a man who had the power of the LORD in his pocket not scoff at such a threat? But Elijah had nothing left in him, not even faith.

"Then he was afraid; he got up and fled for his life, and came to Beer-sheba, which belongs to Judah; he left his servant there. But he himself went a day's journey into the wilderness, and came and sat down under a solitary broom tree."

"He asked that he might die: 'It is enough; now, O LORD, take away my life, for I am no better than my ancestors.' Then he lay down under the broom tree and fell asleep." (1 Kings 19:3-5)

Can you imagine The Rock wallowing like this after blowing up the bad guys? No way. We like our superheroes tough and wise-crackin'—Bruce Willis as Elijah would look toward the horizon where the rain cloud was about to form and raise an impish brow, "Can I offer anyone a drink?" But as for weakness, exhaustion, vulnerability, we prefer that be limited to a scrape on the forehead, a smear of dirt on a cheek, maybe a sling put on by a paramedic, who the alpha male then pushes aside to go kiss the girl. We want to know that, unlike us, our heroes can defeat a city of enemies then go have a few beers and a good night's sleep, usually not alone.

It was to obliterate the image of heroes such as this that God became human and gave us a new model, one who knows the dark night of the soul, who has already been to the blackest place and lived to tell about it. Because none of us, no matter how strong or smart or beautiful or rich or funny or wise or powerful, will get through our lives without periods of utter exhaustion, helplessness, even despair. Many will have thoughts of suicide; some will even attempt it and, with increasing frequency, succeed. In the United States, someone kills him or herself every 17 minutes, and the rates are on the rise, nowhere more than in the group between the ages of 15 and 24.

In the fall of 2010, we as a nation were forced to look at the unique and excruciating pain of our gay teens, who are literally slashing themselves in the hopes that we will listen: in the first five weeks of Remy's junior year, six gay American teenagers committed suicide to escape chronic and relentless taunting. Even those who opposed gay marriage in the state of California were saying "enough." A new campaign rose up from the masses of gay and lesbian adults—*It Gets Better*—featuring happy, successful homosexuals describing what they had endured as teenagers, trying to save these young souls who hear no other message than who they are is not ok. Most teenagers, gay or straight, hip or nerdy, popular or unpopular, feel this way at some point or another; that they are somehow just not right. I can't imagine that we do anything to lessen their suspicions when we insist they perform at certain numeric levels and with uniform excellence. It is, at its core, a message based in fear that we couch in the language of love (we're only doing it for you!). But each time we force them into a test-prep course or another AP class, force them to develop impressive, externally-driven passions, raise a

153

judgmental brow at their B+ papers, gladly refill their Adderall prescriptions so they can study a little harder, what could we possibly be telling them other than who they are and what they seem to be capable of on their own simply will not cut it?

What is it we want for them, really? Let's be honest. If what we really want, more than just some fuzzy notion of happiness, is for them to make lots of money (despite the fact that decades of research prove that, beyond having needs met, wealth does nothing to improve levels of happiness) then we should seriously consider this: there are well-documented traits that will increase someone's likelihood of being wealthy and most of them are 100% beyond our control. Good looks, height, and being born into a family that already has money: these are the three leading precursors to wealth. Ironically, the issue of intelligence makes a minimal difference: Yes, those with high IQs will likely have a greater annual earning potential, but their ability to hold onto or accumulate wealth is only 1.5 times greater than those of low intelligence. If your child is like most kids—average height, appearance, and family income—you would be better off nurturing their entrepreneurial instincts (which include original thinking, risk-taking, and failure) than ramrodding them into a prestigious academic path.

And if you really, really want your children to be set for life, you won't be able to ignore this key statistic: the biggest determining factor of lifelong financial prosperity is marriage. Just that. Getting married and staying married. Sometimes I think that our glib and breezy views on divorce have helped to fuel our high earnings frenzy, as if we see it as inevitable that our kids will need to be able to afford to divvy up their adult income over a few different homes. But lifelong commitments and the accompanying emotional support are not simply a matter of finances. Not only will staying married increase wealth by 77% over a lifetime, it will put you in the lowest group for suicide risk in the nation.

For years, communities of faith of all kinds contributed to the shame surrounding suicide and added to the suffering of those left behind. Today, all the world's religions are joining forces in showing compassion to those who suffer and stepping up their support to prevent suicide at all costs. The desire to end one's life is not a simple matter. It is born of hopelessness, guilt, shame, desperation, self-loathing, and weariness. There is almost always an element of mental illness, and often of substance abuse, as well. Although many think that suicide is an irreversible decision, the evidence shows otherwise. Oftentimes even the smallest acts of caring, of time, of feeling connected to a loving community can see someone through their dark nights of the soul, particularly in teenagers, who are prone to myopic thinking and the inability to see beyond the next bell.

Elijah never had the luxury of that kind of community. He was a loner by trade and prone to dark thoughts. He was called to enter into conflict and surround himself with his known enemies. He was called to live alone and wait. Even a servant of the LORD can suffer the demons of despair. His nerves racked with adrenalin and

155

exhaustion and the aftermath of having the full power of the living God shoot through his body like lightning as he declared His truth and prepared His stage, he lay down under a tree and asked to die. Not unlike so many young people today—and, as our winnowing economy drags on, their parents, as well—who feel that they've done the best they can, that it isn't enough, that it never will be, that the attacks just keep on coming, that they simply can't go on.

"Suddenly, an angel touched him and said to him, 'Get up and eat.' Elijah looked, and there at his head was a cake baked on hot stones, and a jar of water. He ate and drank, and lay down again."
"The angel of the LORD came a second time, touched him, and said, 'Get up and eat, otherwise the journey will be too much for you.' He got up, and ate and drank." (1 Kings 19: 5-8)

Remy and I were both exhausted. Five years of skating in the mornings, of getting up in the dark and preparing for the day ahead with Tupperware containers of healthy snacks, homework folders, changes of clothes, textbooks, water bottles, skate jackets, calculators, yearbook checks, permission slips, dioramas in the rain: the days were long and always, for me, accompanied by the twisted knowledge that this was a lot of time and energy to put into anything. She needed sleep. We both did. Everything is harder without rest.

God knows that better than any of us. When Elijah feels he can't go on, God doesn't say "Get up! You're falling behind!" He sends an angel to offer him rest and hydration and the sweet sustenance of a warm grain cake. (Really, is there any sorrow or fatigue that can't be improved upon by a little cake?). And God doesn't say "Hurry up and eat your snack, daylight's a-wasting!" He says "rest, and rest some more."

We know the facts: teenagers need a minimum of nine hours of sleep a night. During adolescence their circadian rhythms are reset, telling them to fall asleep later at night and wake up later in the morning. The change is brought on by a hormone—melatonin, to be exact—which is produced in the body later at night in teens than it is in kids and adults. Lack of sleep has a serious impact on memory, concentration, mood, and overall effectiveness— we all know this—and yet—tick, tock— if a teenager today wants a shot at a good college, they will not only have to shine academically, but show that they are model citizens, investing considerable time in community service work, ideally something they created on their own, as well as being exceptional at an extracurricular activity. It's no longer enough to captain of the swim team; our kids need to be swimming the English Channel in world record time while simultaneously acing their APs, SATs, ACTs, GPAs, and delousing refugee dogs from Haiti, all at a time when what they really need most is a nice long nap. How can we possibly afford to let them spend those precious minutes sleeping when all those other parents are telling their kids that they can sleep all they want once they've made it to the top? Loving parents that we are, we pull back the covers, set the bars, hold the stopwatches, check off the months, the minutes, the scores, record the numbers in what our kids had been told again and again and again—I heard you!!!—is their permanent record. Tick, tock.

There is a wonderful watch shop near us where we've had occasion to go over the years. The strap on Lon's tide watch had broken in a south swell last week, and he needed it fixed before a trip. I was in the store for about a half hour and in that time four men came in, each one of them wanting a strap fixed. None of them stopped to browse the beautiful new watches in the case; all of us trying to make what we have last a little bit longer.

I have only worn a watch one time in my life. I had gotten it before I went off to college, certain that there would be all sorts of last minute dashing and jetting from quad to classroom. I was a smoker back then and even more compulsive than I am now. Within a month I found myself checking the watch between minutes. I began to time things: three minutes for this cigarette, two minutes to go to the bathroom, six minutes to walk to class, plus a five minute cushion. I dread being late. Even then, at 17, I knew this slavishness to time was not serving me. I put the watch in the drawer and haven't worn one since.

For Graham's 20th birthday, this was his one request: a good watch. I stood to the side as he looked discerningly at the selections. He began with watches that seemed, to me, appropriate for his age and lifestyle—a college kid who coached baseball and wore shorts a lot—but then started to gravitate towards sleeker, more sensuous models. Graphite with angles and sheen. Watches worn by men with business dinners to attend—in Luxembourg. The owner was a handsome young craftsman who wore an Italian suit and a silver optical loop on a chain around his neck, evoking thoughts of Florence and the artisan movement. He laid the choices out on a velvet pad for Graham to consider.

"This one seems more like you," I said, tapping the band of the sports model.

"I'm really liking this one," he said, again asking to try on one of the stylish European models. The price difference was not great enough to make that the issue.

"Doesn't that kind of seem like a lot of watch for a 20-year old?" I said, attempting to enlist the support of the owner.

"It depends on the 20-year old," he said.

After years of coming in, I had seen that his only angle was to make sure that the purchaser loved their watch the way he loved all timepieces. He was an anachronism to me; all elegance and Old World care in a mini mall between a Thai Bar-b-cue shop and a dry cleaner's. I had asked him his story one time. He had come to that watch shop as a teenager and apprenticed with an old watchmaker who taught him everything he knew about his craft, the sorts of things that can only be taught one person to another. He had young children and set his hours to be around for all their special events. He did a useful thing well and there were always people in the store happy to pay for his services.

"Mom, I really think I want this one," Graham said definitively.

"OK," I relented, reminding him to keep it in the case when he wasn't wearing it (because, really, how often could a college student wear a watch like that?). I didn't want it to get scratched or broken or worse—stolen.

"I think I'll wear it a lot," he said.

Over the past year, I've never seen it off him. When he went to work all summer at an internship that required him to wear slacks and a dress shirt, he was in his element. Daily, he wrote articles and press releases. He was allowed to sit in on meetings with key executives making major decisions. He described for me the corner office of the CEO in detail. And I realized, as I stood in the shop now, waiting for Lon's new rubber watchband—the kind that made him feel like him—that Graham had chosen a watch that fit the man he planned to be, and wearing it each day had helped him become that.

With the prevalence of smart phones, and digital clocks on every corner, watches have become utterly ornamental. I wondered as I waited if they would end up going the way of pay phones and soon, newspapers, or if they would always be the sort of prop that would help a man define himself. The owner moved swiftly, without haste, stopping to demonstrate for his young apprentice a tiny, calibrated trick of the trade, and in doing so, slowed the world to the pace of a teachable moment: repairing time.

"Then Elijah went in the strength of that food forty days and forty nights to Horeb, the mount of God. At that place, he came to a cave, and spent the night there." (1 Kings 19:8-9)

The LORD had revived Elijah with food and water and rest. Still, it was not time for him to jump back in the hot seat. After a season of rest comes a season of contemplation. Forty days and forty nights. A recurring length of biblical time, the most well known of which is Lent. Lent is the season of reflection that leads up to Easter. It is a time to consider the meaning of one's faith, to give up habits that we have come to rely on for comfort and joy more than God. In our own contemporary way we are recreating, in those forty days, Moses' mountaintop moments, the sequestering of Elijah, and temptation of Christ, who went into the wilderness to do battle with Satan, who offered Him riches and power and, as time wore on, food and water. This is when Christ responds for the first time, **"Man does not live by bread alone."**

We tend to forget that. Forget to take time to feed our spiritual dimension, to teach our children to feed and nurture theirs. We ask them to go from mountaintop moment to mountaintop moment with little more than a Red Bull in between. It's no wonder there is an epidemic, not only of cheating, but of speed-based drug use to assist in cramming, as well. On college campuses of every stripe, and increasingly in suburban high schools, the use of ADD meds to make it possible to study 18 hours straight is becoming standard practice. No one expects that any information will actually be retained from this method, that any real learning will occur—that's hardly the point. It's the grade, stupid, just the grade that counts. That, and a killer internship which has now replaced the lazy, hazy summer job, where kids used to learn about making milk shakes and friends, and in the wee hours, when it was too hot to sleep, to begin to imagine who they might be when they grow up.

In the capstone class of my management program, we were asked to write a 10-page paper encapsulating where we'd been, what we'd learned, and where we planned to go next. On the syllabus it indicated that the paper would need to be vetted through the online plagiarism checker. This was standard practice—a sign of the times, sadly—but I couldn't imagine it applied to this assignment. I wrote to the instructor with a humorous query: You don't really think someone is going to rip off his own life story, do you? He replied quickly: I've had it happen dozens of times. Kids will cut and paste an entire life, formative years, influences, passions, goals, all without batting an eye. What possible purpose would that serve? I wondered, but didn't need to answer my own question. In forcing our kids to focus only on the result, we've taken the value of self-reflection right out of the equation.

Chapter 11

After 40 days, when Elijah reached the mount of God, he came to a cave and spent the night there. **"Then the word of the LORD came to him, saying, 'What are you doing here, Elijah?'"**

He answered, **"I have been very zealous for the LORD, the God of hosts; for the Israelites have forsaken your covenant, thrown down your altars, and killed your prophets with the sword. I alone am left, and they are seeking my life, to take it away."** (1 Kings 19: 9-10)

I can hear my own voice in his as Elijah declares all the wrong things that "they" have done, and that he, poor, put-out soul, is alone in fighting the good fight. He pleads for God to intervene, and if he's like most of us—like me, certainly—he hopes that the LORD will finally come down and say, "You are my beloved child. Couldn't have done it without you."

Fighting the good fight can be lonely business. It often appears that no one else cares about doing the right thing. But from a God's eye view, we discover that there are

163

as many righteous warriors as there are good fights. While Elijah had been called to speak truth to power, the LORD had others working on separate pieces of the grand design. Remember Obadiah, Ahab's chief of staff? Well he revered the LORD so greatly that when Jezebel started killing off God's prophets, he went out and hid 100 of them—50 to a cave—and kept them alive all through the drought. What do we imagine they were doing all those years? Removed from earthly concerns, they were free to pray and rest and listen for new visions for the future; when Elijah was on his last legs, a whole troop of fresh and reverent prophets could emerge to speak on God's behalf. Greater still, as the LORD will soon reveal, there are 7000 people that Elijah seems to know nothing about who have resisted bowing down to Baal and have been meeting all along to pray in secret to the living God. And, as we will soon discover, there is another young prophet—not Elijah, but Elisha—whom the LORD has silently prepared to take the prophet's mantle, his Word and truth carrying on unbroken through all the ages.

In this moment, Elijah can see none of this. All he knows is he's given his whole life to the service of God and now it seems he's going to have to spend his remaining days on the lamb from a blood-thirsty queen. Really? Is that how you want to play this, God? After all I've done for you? To Elijah, his life has become a private battle reduced to a single fight. It is this self-obsessed tunnel vision that blinds us all to wider possibilities. The same tunnel vision that leads even sensible parents to believe that if their kids don't get into The Chosen One pre-school, they will never get into Best and Brightest Elementary, or Cut Above High, and their chances of having the sort of university credentials that will set the stage for an important life will be reduced to a crapshoot. We imagine that everyone is buying into this win-at-all-costs-mania because so many are. But many is not all.

In the year after Remy had her brain surgery, Lon and I would go out to the occasional movie. There was a seventh grader named Elizabeth, who babysat for several of the church and school families. She was a bright, wholesome, fresh-scrubbed girl, all knees and elbows and smiles. As my kids grew up, I watched as she walked the streets to Venice High, earned swim team honors, covered her nose with zinc oxide for her summer duties as a lifeguard in Santa Monica. When she left for UC Davis, I would see her at church on Christmas Eve and smiled as she grew into a young woman, and Graham began to pass her by in height. Her father was a lawyer and her sister had become one, too. I would soon discover that Elizabeth had followed in their footsteps, a strange choice I thought: nothing in her spirit felt to me compatible with a life of practicing law.

I ran into her the other day at the doctor's office. She looked beautiful and happy and was accompanied by a very handsome, surfery-looking guy. He was called in for his check-up, leaving us to talk.

"Is it serious?" I smiled, always hungry for news of love.

"I don't know, yet," she said. "But I'm really, really happy."

"Is he a lawyer?"

"Oh, no, he's a lifeguard."

"Really? The lawyer and the lifeguard. Sounds like a perfect match."

"Oh, no, I'm not a lawyer anymore. Well, at least not now."

She went on to tell me that, after placing top in her class, she had chosen to go to work for the D.A. One year of seeing up close what the system was all about, the entrenched politics and the culture of crime and poverty and the utter inability to effect any real change on the lives of people, was enough to convince her that this was not her Calling. She decided to take a year off, returning to the lifeguarding job she'd had all through high school and college. She imagined she'd take a little time to regroup, but found that the money was sufficient to cover the cost of her apartment and she was happy and healthy and in love and for now that was more than enough.

I have no idea if she'll practice law again or not, but I do know that she is listening to a voice that is bigger and wiser and more powerful than numbers. She's not alone in that. The other day my friend Sarah turned me on to a small, local food specialty company called Josie's English Kitchen. The woman makes wonderful chutneys and relishes and tampenades—the sorts of things that make for perfect fall and winter meals. Trolling through the website, I discovered that Josie had an MA in Theatre Arts and an MA in Divinity, neither of which seem to be prerequisites for the making of chutney.

The circuitous route is not an uncommon path for women. Our children tend to draw us in, closer to the hearth, closer to the heartbeat of community. Many of us refashion our lives around their worlds and, in doing so, find a deeper joy. For some, this is made possible by having a husband with a decent job. Curiously, this was the original model for the family unit—husband as provider, wife as caretaker, both as partners in life and love, dedicated to each other's happiness and the well-being of their children. Today, I know more women than men who are the sole breadwinners of the family and, for all their ability and success and accomplishment, it doesn't feel quite right to them. Secretly, and sometimes not so secretly, they'd rather it be the other way around.

There is always a price to pay for progress. Yes, our daughters now have every door open to them, but our sons are failing out of school in ever increasing numbers. Yes, we have wives supporting upper-middle class families, but what has happened to their husbands as they slowly age and lose their power? Many experts agree that the female management style is superior to the male's—more consensus building, more nurturing, better at developing talent and instilling loyalty—kind of like being a good mom. Some men have developed these skills as well, but most are still victims of their own kill-or-be-killed natures, the very natures we once valued so much when it came to providing food or protecting nations. I'm not sure that all the theories of gender and hormones are etched in stone. One look at the women who appeared on a recent California ballot—Meg Whitman, Carly Fiorina, Barbara Boxer—and you'll see that any hint of apron strings has been left behind to win in a man's world.

When I returned to work a few years ago, I was thrown into situations with several high-powered women who have gone on to make multi-million dollar salaries and would chew you up and spit you out before they'd risk a penny of it. There was a chill in their presence reminiscent of Jezebel, a woman who ran the castle, had the king pussywhipped, and lured an entire nation of faithful Jews into deserting the LORD in favor of her instant-gratification-more-goodies-for me gods. There was a time I thought that more women in leadership would be a good thing, but now I wonder if it is not a matter of male or female, but of motive. Few people are actually Gifted to be leaders, but many aspire to do so. When we aspire to be what we are not, we corrupt the grace of the tasks at hand and the whole bloody process turns evil.

One of the blessings of church life is that it forces you into community with people you are unlikely to spend time with otherwise. Because of this, we are granted an opportunity to expand our breadth of compassion and understanding. Over the past few years, I have become increasingly aware of the plight of men in their fifties and sixties whom the world has already rejected. It is too late for them to mount another big push at something grand. For many of them, their wounded egos and inflexible natures have kept them from adapting. They are angry and growing poorer and still can't figure out how the world has turned on them this way; they, for the most part, good men, who didn't see the new world order coming.

Where would we have these men go to find love and belonging? The Bowl-a-rama? Starbucks? Is that where we would want our kids to turn when their lives unravel in middle age? It's a question worth asking. We, of the coastal elite, who have trained our children to think of God and the church as foolish, antiquated, a crutch for the weak or a training ground for the hateful, have made it all but impossible for them to seek solace here. For all our talk of peace and bi-partisanship, we adore our distinctions of us and them. For all our degrees and book club smarts, we're blind to the fact that we, and our children, could one day be cautionary tales in a story that's much bigger than any one of us.

Consider the parable of the Good Samaritan. It begins with a man seeking to inherit eternal life—the ultimate prize—and Jesus telling him how it will be accomplished.

"You shall love the Lord your God with all your heart, and with all your soul, and with all your strength, and with all your mind; and your neighbor as yourself."

The man then asks Jesus, **"And who is my neighbor?"** Jesus answered, as he often did, with a parable.

"A man was going down from Jerusalem to Jericho, and fell into the hands of robbers, who stripped him, beat him, and went away, leaving him half dead. Now by chance a priest was going down that road: and when he saw him, he passed by on the other side. So likewise a Levite, when he came to the place and saw him, passed by on the other side."

"But a Samaritan while traveling came near him; and when he saw him, he was moved with pity. He went to him and bandaged his wounds, having poured oil and wine on them. Then he put him on his own animal, brought him to an inn, and took care of him."

"The next day he took out two denarii, gave them to the innkeeper, and said, 'Take care of him; and when I come back, I will repay you whatever more you spend.' Which of these three, do you think, was a neighbor to the man who fell in to the hands of the robbers?' He said, 'The one who showed him mercy.'"

"Jesus said to him, 'Go and do likewise.'" (Luke 10:27-37)

Most of us have probably heard some version of the story, maybe even paused to think about what we'd do in that situation. We'd like to think that we would stop and help, but if we're honest with ourselves we know that a lot would depend on the day, on whether or not we were late for work or school or if the man looked as if he might be diseased. For most of us, the story is simply about whether or not we would choose to be a good guy or a bad guy—but look closer. There are actually five archetypes in the story: the man who helps, the two men who don't, the innkeeper who agrees to assist, and the man in a heap on the side of the road, the one character to whom we rarely give a second thought. When the scripture is reduced to folklore, which it often is, there is a tendency to morph the image of that man into a sad, dirty lump of his own creation, but that's not what the story says. The man had simply been walking down the road when he was robbed, stripped, and beaten.

Think about it. If he were robbed, he must have started out on the journey with something of value—a nice Swiss watch, perhaps. His clothes must have been worth something, too, either in their finery or their necessary warmth. He was on the same road that both high priests and ordinary outcast Samarians travelled—Wilshire Blvd., or the like. In other words, his bad fortune was not, in any way, his fault.

Some folks delight in this story because the religious men reveal themselves to be hypocrites, and it is the common man with a heart of gold that comes to the rescue. And they are right to take note of those things. I know many non-religious people who do a life of good work, and I think we're all aware of religious leaders—or those who purport to lead on God's behalf—that do more harm than good. But Jesus was never one for handy stereotypes. Nor was he one to let us cherry pick the parts of the lessons we liked best—no, he wants us to consider the whole of the story and all its challenges. And that means accepting the fact that each one of us, and each one of our children, will at some point in our lives, be the person who is beaten up and left for scrap, whether literally or figuratively, and there is no right road that will prevent it.

We, the culture of the self-made man, tend not to talk about that, as if being vulnerable is something that can be outsmarted. It can't. Since the dawn of man, each and every one of us has been only one crushed vertebrae, one unrequited love, one dark alley, one mottled cell, one blown megadeal away from being less than we had planned. And it is only in the recognition of that common weakness that we begin to find our way home.

Henry has been coming around more than usual lately. He likes to have cereal with us in the morning while his mom or dad takes Freja to school. He still loves to run and play and ride his Razor down the steepest driveway, but there is something wounded in him; he doesn't want to go back to preschool, not now, not yet. He has nightmares; they all do. He's terrified of elevators and trash trucks and Zambonis. Miracles can help us skirt death but not the impact near tragedy makes on our spirits. We carry our wounds and our scars with us for life. Maybe this is why we are so determined to swaddle our children in cushions and pads and helmets; to bolster them with enrichment and tutoring, to immunize them with classical music and trips to the theatre, to bludgeon them into becoming a living, breathing transcript that can transcend most any rejection, all so they can avoid the sting of ending up at a college where, for the rest of their lives when they say the name, no one will look impressed. Are we sure we aren't making too much of that? College admissions officers say we are, reporting loudly and to anyone who will listen, that kids who go off to their third or fourth or fifth choice school settle in just fine and within weeks can't imagine being anywhere else.

In the Buddhist faith there is a belief that desire is the root of all suffering. I think they might be right.

Whether our desire is for wealth or power or the misleading benevolence of claiming we just want our kids to be happy, these are the things that will cause us to suffer—sometimes because we didn't get what we wanted, and sometimes because we did. But the Buddhist approach asks us to transcend suffering, and that is where I respectfully part ways. I have come to see that the only way to transcend suffering is to enter into a relationship with the One who became suffering incarnate, who joined us in our pain and loss, who joins us each day if we let him, and lifts us from the quicksand into new life. In the words of Simone Weil, the Jewish mystic who was called to Christ, "The extreme greatness of Christianity lies in the fact that it does not seek a supernatural remedy for suffering but a supernatural use for it."

We can only teach what we know. This weekend, Henry and Freja were helping me bake pumpkin pies. My aunt taught me to bake when I was little. I would sleep over at their house on the weekends and we'd make waffles and sweet rolls and cookies and cake. I learned to measure just like Fannie Farmer, and to sort the dry and wet ingredients. I learned to use a flour sifter and a rolling pin and a whisk. I learned to separate eggs and guesstimate dashes. I learned to steady the bowl as the batter spun in the big professional-looking metal mixer, and to check for doneness with a wooden toothpick, and to wrap pecans in cheesecloth and crush them with a mallet. I learned to love baking because I sat at the feet of someone who loved baking, and me. After living half a century, I honestly believe this is the only learning that ever really sticks.

Our neighbor Tim was a physics major. He confessed to me that he spends hours of his free time on geeksquad.com trolling for ideas to make science come to life. He can't wait till his kids are old enough to share what he knows. I told him that he doesn't have to wait, that we'll work him into the syllabus at the Davis Academy. What I don't tell him is that there are no guarantees that his kids will love what he loves; in fact, he'd be wise not to count on it. It was inconceivable to Lon that his children would not grow up to love surfing, his greatest passion, but neither of them have ever shown any interest or aptitude. Remy has grown up with two parents who love to read and a mother who loves to write, but I could tell from the day she was born that she would never like reading. Even the simplest board books bored her. Graham and I made reading tents and sat in the shadows with stacks of books that he clamored for more of. I could no more make her love books than I could make him hate them.

Graham sent me a message last night. The dream of building a life out of his love of sports seems to be waning slightly and in its stead is a new fire for writing. A crossfade was in play. Each week his power with language grows stronger, and now in the evenings he finds himself entertaining storylines and character threads, studiously watching entire seasons of the best written shows in television—Breaking Bad, Mad Men, Friday Night Lights, Modern Family—tuning his ear for pitch perfect dialogue, noting when a character's actions seem inconsistent. At 21, he is now starting to know himself and what he wants and how to get it. Baseball had given him joy and a work ethic and a sense of his own worth. Pitching had taught him perseverance and how to cope with loss. If he wanted to be a writer, he'd need those skills as much as anything else.

When I was little, my dad used to tell me that a girl like me could grow up to be President. I knew it was supposed to make me feel good and important and capable, and I loved him for that, but when I became nothing of the sort, it was hard not to wonder if I was supposed to live a more impressive life. This is the curse we pass on to our children when we continue to warp the intent of the American trope that "anyone can grow up to be President." It was intended as a counterpoint to the presumed elitism that prevented any but wealthy white men from rising to the ultimate power, but we have twisted the word *can* into the shape of the sentiment *anything you can do, I can do better.* As if being President is now a goal that anyone can, and therefore should, aspire to. Had I listened to my dad, gone to the Mirman School for the Highly Gifted, then on to Stanford, his alma mater, then on to law school or B-school or some sort of graduate program in public policy with an eye towards someone else's idea of greatness, I would have found myself, in middle age, exceedingly well dressed yet writhing in my skin from the painful awareness that I was not in my right House. Sooner or later, the truth of who we are insists on having its due:

Dante captured it in the opening of his *Inferno*, "Midway through the journey of our life I came to myself in a dark wood, for the straight way was lost…"

May Sarton expressed it this way: "Now I become myself. It's taken time, many years and places. I have been dissolved and shaken, worn other people's faces…"

And in the words of the poet Mary Oliver, "One day you finally knew what you had to do, and began, though the voices around you kept shouting their bad advice—though the whole house began to tremble and you felt the old tug at your ankles…"

In a famous old Hasidic tale, cited in Parker Palmer's *Let Your Life Speak*, the Rabbi Zusya distills the truth of our lives down to this: "In the coming world, they will not ask me: 'Why were you not Moses?' but rather, 'Why were you not Zusya?'"

Finally, C.S. Lewis, in *The Problem of Pain*, shows us how to think of our God-given individuality in a whole new light:

"….I am considering not how, but why, He makes each soul unique. If He had no use for all these differences, I do not see why He should have created more souls than one. Be sure that the ins and outs of your individuality are no mystery to Him; and one day they will no longer be a mystery to you. The mould in which a key is made would be a strange thing, if you had never seen a key: and the key itself a strange thing if you had never seen a lock. Your soul has a curious shape because it is a hollow made to fit a particular swelling in the infinite contours of the Divine substance, or a key to unlock one of the doors in the house with many mansions. For it is not humanity in the abstract that is to be saved, but you."

The wisdom of the ages is all there for us to draw from. Why, then, do we find it so hard to teach these lessons to our children? Maybe because it requires relinquishing control, not only to our kids, but to a God we don't want to believe in. Maybe because our own egos are so fragile we cannot bear to give our lives to the raising of children only to have them become ordinary people. There, I said it. The worst thing a 21st-century child of interesting parents could be: ordinary. Like us. So we fluff them and fold them and nudge them and enhance them and bind them and break them and embellish them beyond measure; then, as we drive them up to the college interviews that they've heard since birth are the gateway to the lives they were destined to lead based on nothing more than our own need for it to be true, we tell them, with a smile so tight it would crack nuts, "Just be yourself."

Chapter 12

Then God said to Elijah: **"Go out and stand on the mountain before the LORD, for the LORD is about to pass by. Now there was a great wind, so strong that it was splitting mountain and breaking rocks in pieces before the LORD, but the LORD was not in the wind; and after the wind an earthquake, but the LORD was not in the earthquake: and after the earthquake a fire, but the LORD was not in the fire and after the fire a sound of sheer silence."** (1 Kings 19:11-13)

Always we return to silence. If we want answers greater than our own noisy perspectives, this is where they will be found. In this new revelation in the Elijah narrative we see God's point: yes, I can split mountains and move the air with monumental force, and shake the foundations of the earth and call down fire—on Moses' bush, on Elijah's bull, in the hearts of believers—whenever and wherever I choose. But I am not just a God out there, but in here. Listen.

Over the years, I've developed a healthy fear of media and technology's ability to consume our silence. I have learned it firsthand. I know that once I turn on my shows at night, God would have to revert to the old earthquake method to get my attention. Once I allowed email and Facebook to become a part of my daily life, I was susceptible to the same nervous twitch as the most enslaved crackberry user. That's why Lon and I have never allowed the kids to have TVs or computers in their rooms. They watch and engage in media in other rooms, usually with us, but we know that they will have their hours of silent alone time. This is their training ground for a life without me or Lon or some external voice of who or what they should be, want, do.

When Graham was in pre-school the Director called me aside one day at pickup. She wanted to share something that had happened. Graham had been out on the yard riding trikes with his friends, playing, happy. He was always an easy-going kid, no drama, no conflicts. Then, suddenly he went up to his teacher and said he felt he needed a little quiet time and would it be ok to just go up in the reading loft in the room and be by himself for a little while? The Director said that in all her years she had never had a child ask to do that. While other parents might take that as a sign for alarm, I took it as the greatest affirmation of his young life.

When I was pregnant with Graham, Lon recalled a book he had read in high school called *Summerhill*. It was written by a radical British child development pioneer, A. S. Neill, who founded a boarding school based on the simple principle that an education should be based not on academic achievement, but on a child's own definition of success. Strange book, I thought, for a teenage boy from a military family in the south to be reading for fun in high school. But its truths must have spoken to Lon's heart, the lesson that a child will always seek to learn that which is important to him and that, left to his own devices, he will learn more, not less. The classes at Summerhill, which is still an active boarding school today, are all optional. Students attend when and if they please, which sounds like a recipe for anarchy, but quite the opposite has been proven there over the last 90 years. The students who come pay attention, are eager to learn, and take ownership of the material. There are often many ages represented in a given class, as children develop at their own pace and not in keeping with an imposed timeline. Freed of the Sisyphean boulder of requirements, they cultivate a sense of knowing themselves—their interests, gifts, talents, curiosities—and pursue work that supports them. Upon graduation, the students are not only equally well prepared for college study, they are emotionally far more mature than most teenagers. "The aim of life," Neill says, "is to find happiness, which means to find interest. Education should be a preparation for life."

Remy has been home for a month now and I have already found this to be true. Each week I give her a syllabus of work, and she uses it as a guideline. I signed her up for the same online math program I had used to test all the way through 6 units of college math. ALEKS.com is her new addiction. In the first few weeks I tried to tell her she should do her math first each day, as I had, get it out of the way.

"Worst for first, mom," she would tell me.

"Exactly," I replied.

"But math is not worst for me. Reading is. I like doing math anytime of day."

Last night around 10:00, I found her on the computer and, certain that she was on Facebook, told her to go to bed. She responded brightly that she was in the middle of a math assessment. Me, I could barely count how many minutes were left in the hour but for Remy, evidently, algebraic equations are like a nice cup of chamomile tea.

"...and after the fire a sound of sheer silence. When Elijah heard it, he wrapped his face in his mantle and went out and stood at the entrance of the cave. Then there came a voice to him that said, 'What are you doing here, Elijah?'" (1 Kings 19:11-13)

It's a funny thing for God to ask. He knows what Elijah is doing there. He just wants to hear how he'll frame it. And Elijah frames it the way most of us would: we say the same thing we've already said (we just love to beat those dead horses) and emphasize, *again*, just how righteous we are. Allow me to translate:

"Elijah answered (again!)**, 'I have been very zealous for the LORD, the God of hosts...'"**

This is sort of a biblical variation on "I'm your biggest fan." Not too original, but I'm not sure any of us would do any better. At least Elijah knew to say something nice before he started complaining.

"For the Israelites have forsaken your covenant, thrown down your altars, and killed your prophets with the sword..."

"Again, just in case you haven't been paying attention, God, let me recap. I'm the good guy and everyone else is the bad guy. They are not your biggest fans. They didn't even see your last three movies. And they haven't just been faithless, they've been abhorrent."

The next interesting thing is what Elijah doesn't say, skipping from **"killed your prophets with a sword"** to this, **"I alone am left."** Notice anything missing? Say, the 100 prophets hiding in the caves? But wait, you say, Elijah doesn't know anything about them, right? Wrong. Obadiah told Elijah all about them when they met face to face right before the Showdown. Is it possible that Elijah already forgot that there were actually other people who have the same Gift that he has? Who, as he speaks, are snuggled 50 to a cave hanging out, bonding, not unlike the Chilean miners, praying and fellowshipping with nothing but fanfare and their own talk shows waiting on the outside—but not Elijah. No. Elijah had to do his work alone. And so he says, part pitying, part aggrandizing, part threat:

"I alone am left. And they are seeking my life, to take it away."

In case God misses the implication: "I'm all you've got, and if they kill me, you won't have a single living soul left on Earth to help you." Got to admire his chutzpah on that one. But the LORD is not into false praise or atta boys:

183

he will answer Elijah's cry for help and relief in three ways far more valuable than compliments.

First, He proclaims several key changes, effective immediately, in leadership in the Northern Kingdom. (So Elijah will know that his work has not been in vain). He reveals to Elijah that there are actually quite a few people— 7000, to be exact—who have resisted the false prophets during his time (which should serve both as reassurance and a call to humility). And finally, He announces the name of his successor, (so Elijah can look forward to his rest, free from the worry that his good work will not be carried on). Flattery is nice, but proof of having made a difference is better. So is being given the honor of having a glimpse of the big picture. Here it is:

"The LORD said to him, 'Go, return on your way to the wilderness of Damascus; when you arrive, you shall anoint Hazael, as king over Aram.'"

"Also you shall anoint Jehu son of Nimshi as king over Israel; and you shall anoint Elisha son of Shaphat of Abel-meholah as prophet in your place."

"Whoever escapes from the sword of Hazael, Jehu shall kill; and whoever escapes from the sword of Jehu, Elisha shall kill."

"Yet I will leave seven thousand in Israel, all the knees that have not bowed to Baal, and every mouth that has not kissed him." (1 Kings 19:15-18)

What I notice most is the incredible efficiency and obvious hierarchy in the marching orders. Even in a land that appears to be run by godless rulers, it's clear that the prophet Elijah is the ultimate human authority. When he anoints these new kings, it is understood that there will be a peaceful transition of power. There is also a clear directive about how to handle any rebellion; Jehu will cover Hazael's back, Elisha will cover Jehu's back.

This sense of hierarchy has been essential to championship sports teams, world-class orchestras, heroic military operations, beneficent administrations, award-winning film crews, the Greek system, the Boy & Girl Scouts, the Red Cross, the L.A. Lifeguards, and the most successful corporations in America—a sense that each person knows to whom they are accountable, and each is accountable ultimately to something greater than themselves. This had been the foundation of America, but it is now so absent from the fabric of our lives as to be considered quaint. The executive organizational model that had defined the most productive years in American life—the sorts of models that were in place when that impressive class of Harvard graduates built businesses without personal agendas—has been all but replaced with a new, flat organizational structure, a model where people seem embarrassed to lead, deferring to some vague notion of everyone playing an equal part.

In my last job as a creative director, I had inherited a team of people who had minimal training for the job they were being asked to do and very little direction as to how to improve their skills. Attempts to create a structure for that growth were met with fierce opposition. Early on, I decided that a weekly team meeting to review the status of people's projects would offer an opportunity to understand the big picture, for each person to become familiar with other accounts and projects, and to offer insight in an open setting that might have some universal benefit. Moments after I sent out the email invite to the new meeting, I received a fairly scathing letter from a very bright and articulate young man informing me that I could not schedule a meeting because I had not asked the members if they felt that a weekly status meeting was a good idea and if they'd be willing to give up half an hour to attend it. He emphasized that for him meetings were "soul sucking" and questioned my right to force him to endure one. Hard to imagine this generation of workers storming the beaches at Normandy.

Without vision, the people perish. Without leadership, management, and direction, it is impossible to disseminate vision. This was the underlying sense I had for most of the two years at the large, rudderless, overly-funded start-up. A series of quarterly directors' meetings was launched, but so many people had been given the title of director in lieu of suitable pay, that three-quarters of the company attended them. Seated in a circle around a large ballroom, it reminded me of my middle school days at cotillion, where we sat around nervously waiting to see who made the first move. I envisioned a rowboat sitting in the middle of a pond—not just at those meetings, but every day on the job—with all the workers circling on shore watching it for movement. The emphasis was on initiative-based thinking, or so I was told when I asked the people who had titles that would define them as upper, upper management if they could bullet point the top three corporate priorities so that I, and others, could make sure our efforts were in sync with their goals. They could not. And so we stood around the pond. If anyone jumped in the boat and started rowing it in any direction, people got excited, then nervous. Fearing they might get left behind, they jumped in the boat and tried to make sure they could find some way to contribute. Unsure of how to align themselves with another person's vision, or to sublimate themselves to anything outside their own comfort zone, they panicked anew, began rowing madly in the opposite direction, not to anywhere in particular, but simply away from any effort that might leave them in the cold.

Hierarchy is a real Goldilocks dilemma. Too much and it becomes bureaucracy, the chains of which prevent reform. Too little, and we have anarchy, the result of a thousand self-absorbed spirits running off in different directions. Organization has become, in our culture, a word synonymous with stuffed shirts, old models, stifled creativity.

The church is accused of this so often that the term "organized religion" is never heard without disdain. I used to use it that way, too. It is the sort of thing a young person has the luxury of saying before he has bills to pay. But after being a church member for 17 years, having served on boards, having looked behind the curtain to see the gears and levers, I know this: churches are buildings supported by people who at some moment in their life felt called by God to know the love of Christ and in finding that love, feel called to be there for others whom God sends their way. They could do it online. They could do it on a street corner. But the model that has been handed down to us is to come together in the flesh in one space, one Body, to praise and worship and grow in the knowledge of God.

And so there will need to be lights and heat and candles and communion wafers, flowers and ushers and coffee and sweets. We organize our lives as a church body so on that one day—any given Sunday—that someone hears the voice of God and decides to walk down the street, confused and uncertain about why they are even there, someone will be there to greet them, to hand them a bulletin with all the words to the songs that will be played so they might follow along; someone else will write them a note afterwards thanking them for coming, suggesting a book or a snippet of scripture that might help with some of the areas of doubt that have kept them away from the church for so long. And a whole group of someones will be silently praying that something that was said or done or felt or heard in that hour was a blessing to the newcomer's heart. The organization of God's church, is, at its best, a beautiful thing.

At its worst, it becomes a playground for powermongers and agenda pushers and those who have fallen just as victim to the message of more, bigger, higher as the secular world. As I write this, the behemoth church known as the Crystal Cathedral here in Anaheim, California has filed for bankruptcy. Many of the top executives received generous payoffs, it seems, before the filing took place. This is not something that makes me happy, but I sense there may be a Godly correction in it. When my first book came out, I was asked to speak at the Crystal Cathedral. It was strange and exciting and what felt like the beginning of big things to come. It wasn't. There were a few dozen people out front who wanted to buy my book, have me sign it, but I was no one special to them. They had writers there every week, each hawking a book, a CD, a series of life-changing seminars.

Talking with my family on the promenade outside, in the shadow of the massive, glass-gleaming church, I saw a giant stone tablet, nearly thirty feet high, and at the top the words: Wall of Christian Capitalists. The term "jumbo shrimp" was instantly supplanted in my mind by this new and utterly incomprehensible oxymoron. The very definition of being a Christian is antithetical to capitalism, at least the form that we now practice in the Orange Counties of this country. To pool resources, energy, and ideas to build some venture that produces jobs, products, and wealth that can then be cycled back into society and apportioned to serve the less fortunate—this, Jesus might buy. He might. But to produce wealth that is held and used for endless personal pleasure, personal aggrandizement, and personal prestige is the description of every evil character in the Bible.

But you can't judge a church by its media profile. Just down the freeway from the Crystal Cathedral is the Saddleback Church, founded by Rick Warren. Over the past 30 years, he has built his small Bible study into a global ministry with 20,000 Sunday worshippers. He has put the idea of living a purpose-driven life on the NY Times bestseller list. He has been called "One of the world's most powerful celebrities" by Forbes Magazine, and by Time, "One of the 100 most influential people in the world." One might be tempted to lump him in with Jim and Tammy

Faye Baker and all the other televangelists who make it so hard for thinking people to believe in The Church. But look again, and you'll see a man who lives in the same home, drives the same car, and puts 90% of his earnings into three charitable ministries: one to help people with AIDS, another to help train leaders in developing nations, and a third, his Global PEACE Fund which uses local congregations to fight the five greatest humanitarian challenges of our time: poverty, disease, corruption, illiteracy, and spiritual emptiness.

"Thus by my fruits you shall know them," says Christ (Matthew 7:20). For those inclined to be contemptuous of organized religion based on nothing more than the rants of a whacked-out relative or the spit and hiss of incendiary media blurbs, I would suggest a field trip to the source someday. Take the kids. We're open Sundays and holidays and most days in between.

When the hierarchical structure is in proper order, there is a natural mentoring relationship in place. One in which the elder listens to the heart of the younger and helps him to discern his path. In which the younger listens to the wisdom of the elder in order to round out his impulses and theoretic studies with life experience. So it is from father to son, from watchmaker to apprentice, from Senior Pastor to Vicar, from Elijah to Elisha.

"So [Elijah] set out from there, and found Elisha son of Shaphat, who was plowing. There were twelve

yoke of oxen ahead of him and he was with the twelfth. Elijah passed by him and threw his mantle over him."

"He left the oxen, ran after Elijah and said, 'Let me kiss my father and my mother, and then I will follow you.'" (1 Kings 19:19-20)

And Elijah waited. If this were a scene in the New Testament, Elisha would not have gotten off so easily. When a newly called disciple says to Jesus, **"Lord, first let me go and bury my father,"** Jesus says to him, **"Follow me, and let the dead bury their own dead."** (Matthew 8:21-22). He is very clear about the significance of a call, and the shift in allegiance from family of origin to family of God. In the family of God, people are placed in our lives to help us realize our full potential whether we like it—or them, or the circumstances—or not. Over the last two decades I have come to recognize that all the growth we could ever hope to experience can come to us through any hundred people of God's choosing. Christ demonstrates this on his final climb to Golgotha. **"Woman, here is your son,"** he says to his mother, and then to one of his disciples, **"Here is your mother."** (John 19:26-27). In this way he provides closure for his loved ones, giving the disciple a sacred duty in the Kingdom, and his mother a young man to care for—to fill the impossible hole.

Without an infrastructure in place to ensure a broad cross-pollination with other lives, ideas, and experiences, our growth becomes stunted. In the western world in the 21st century, young adults form tribes of love and support and we call these, "our new families," and in many ways they are; these are the people we call in the middle of the night through tears. These are the people we share dreams and margaritas with. But there is little balance in these self-selected groups. Without an older angel to oversee our choices, we gravitate towards people just like us, and reject the words of those who don't mimic our own witty thoughts.

I heard a wonderful example of this on a recent retreat to St. Andrews Abbey. Karl, a man I've known for many years, looks like an all-American boy scout all grown up. He is happily married to a lovely Chinese woman he met in college. Their love of Christ and the Chinese culture had become part of their shared life of service. They both work as public school guidance counselors—one high school, one community college—there on the front lines of hell, forced to worry about pink slips even as they struggle to save the very children most likely to be cast off by the new SAT-dominated world order.

Our group was discussing the lessons of identity passed down from our parents. Karl offered to tell a story about his father, a man who had struggled throughout his life with financial stability. On the weekend that the new Getty Center museum opened in Los Angeles, Karl took his father to see it. Even with empty walls, the Getty is an extraordinary place, set high up on a hill. You arrive by a tram that wends through the mountains and delivers you to a tiered platform of travertine marble steps. Glass walls bathe every hall with light and beyond the buildings themselves there is a garden of topiaried flowers and plants—silver spear and canna lily and heliotrope—that provides a true sanctuary from the smog and clamor of the city. Karl led his father into the first building, where room after room of Renoirs and Matisses and Van Goghs were hung with care. His father looked right past them and, pointing directly at the security guard, offered what felt to him like the best advice a father could give a son. "If you're looking for a good job, that's the one right there. All the money this place has, you'd have a steady salary and benefits for life."

We all burst out laughing. Talk about missing the point. But these are the reactions of people who have never suffered true poverty. Upon reflection, a security guard position in a magnificent location that would allow one prone to introspection all the time and mental space he could ever ask for, might, in fact, be a great job. That man could feed his family, spend his days surrounded by beauty and peace, and return home with energy for what he truly loved. Freed of the burden of wondering where his next paycheck would come from, or if his staff of ne'er-do-wells would do their jobs—or scheme to take his—he could spend his time thinking about building a tree house or a gang-prevention program or a winning team of six-year old soccer players—the good, life-giving work done by men who are not madly riding elevators to the top.

If we are willing to set egos aside, the matter comes down to one simple question: how much money do we really need? How many cars, houses, TVs? How many diamonds, facelifts, front row seats? How many bathrooms do our children require in which to brush their precious teeth? And what is the human cost of all that square footage? Of late, we seem to be more concerned about assessing our impact on our natural resources than our human ones. We measure our carbon footprint and make a show of reimbursing the Earth for our ravenous consumption, but not the footprint we make on the psyche of the man who lives down the lane, outside the gate, who only wishes to do something useful with his day and not feel ashamed in front of his family. Where is the algorithm for that? In a world that measures every click-thru, it is hard to imagine that this is merely an oversight, our failure to factor in the societal costs of an executive making 300 times the amount of his company's average worker and how it presses down on the hope and dignity of each and every one of those men. *Those people.* Our neighbors.

Loving One's Neighbor is a line item we've conveniently abolished. In the absence of this beneficent paradigm, we are left popping pills to relieve our unnamed anxieties, to lull us into instant sleep where fits of conscience cannot reach us, and the distant tune of walking a mile in someone else's shoes can fade into a sepia-toned oblivion. I would shout "Wake Up," but I'd be preaching to the choir, wouldn't I? Any thinking, feeling, book-reading person on this good, green earth knows full well that the stratospheric compensation packages of corporate executives in the U.S. today, are, by any humanistic standard, unconscionable. The explanation of why they get away with it—"Because we can"—is an answer that we should no longer accept. These obscene wages—utterly disproportionate to the value of any one man, and rarely matched in profitability—are in no small part the driving force behind the academic frenzy currently eating away at our children and creating a sense of powerlessness and despair in most Americans.

And the blood is on all of our hands. We stood by, each one of us, and let it happen when we chose to idolize not the good man, or the great man, or the courageous man, or the wise man, but the rich man, who we put high on a hill, and gave him full dominion over communities, cultures, his own blind eye-turning Boards, until there were no more checks and balances, no justice, *E pluribus unum* as dead as the language in which it was written; we, as a nation, chose to make The Rich Man our God and now we are all paying the price. **"The love of money is a root of all kinds of evil,"** counsels Paul in his first letter to his protégé, Timothy (1 Timothy 6:10). Curiously, it is in that same letter that the phrase **"fight the good fight"** is first used (1 Timothy 1:18).

For what it's worth, the law is on our side. In 1933, as the people rose up in protest over the corporate greed and negligence that had preceded the Great Depression, and the truth of the staggering executive compensation packages was first revealed (there is nothing new under the sun), shareholders banded together to sue their Boards of Directors. In one such case, *Rogers v. Hill*, the U.S. Supreme Court held that compensation having "no relation to the value of services given" constituted waste. Many had high hopes for the outcome of this trial and its corrective effects but those hopes proved to be as ill-founded as the original SAT creators' dream of finding bright, civic-spirited men to give their all for the common good; *Rogers v. Hill* was settled quietly, out of court, as were many of the cases that followed. To date, in fact, not a single lawsuit challenging executive compensation has been able to prove that any given salary—including Michael Ovitz's $160+ million cash and stock severance package after a failed one-year stint as president of the Walt Disney Company—constituted waste. Edmund Burke taught us that "all that is necessary for evil to triumph is for good men to do nothing," but good men don't feel they have a chance in Hell in this fight. Good fights in America today are expensive.

If ever there was a time for Elijah to return, this is it. So I pray for that prophet, one who can walk into the halls where greed has been allowed to metastasize unchecked, where the nation's new Jezebels have whispered in the ears of weak and willing men, where fear and lust and desire and sloth have led to a monarchy of entitlement, where people in power knowingly inflict harm on the powerless for their own good fortune. Into this realm, the new Elijah must come to say simply, and with ultimate authority, "The party's over."

Pray with me, won't you?

Chapter 13

We cannot make radical change with half-hearted gestures. Change requires risk and pain and confusion and loss along the route to the new good thing. Our mind and hearts cannot move in the direction of the new good thing until our ties to old ways have been severed. Note the very first word spoken by John the Baptist as he endeavored to make a straight path for Christ to enter the hearts of mankind: **"Repent."** Elisha, the young successor, understood that he could not take on the power of Elijah's mantle with one foot still tied to his farm. His call was to a whole new life, one in which he would need to give up being the master of his own fate and become a full-time servant of the LORD. And so Elisha...

"...took the yoke of oxen, and slaughtered them; using the equipment from the oxen, he boiled their flesh, and gave it to the people, and they ate. Then he set out and followed Elijah, and became his servant." (1 Kings 19:21-22)

Elisha's call was not just to a new role in God's kingdom, but a change from stability to uncertainty, from steaks on the grill every night to the promise of nothing more than bird feed. I don't know how anyone could make a change like this without some sort of faith in a benevolent God. Yet, this is the sort of change that our kids will be asked to make as they grow to maturity and leave us. Perhaps our culture of faithlessness accounts for the new phenomenon of helicopter parents who seek to shape and control their children's lives long past childhood. This deviant psychological behavior is not only being seen at the high school and college level but well into graduate school. In 2010, B-school admissions officers found themselves fielding phone calls from overly aggressive parents on a regular basis. Law schools reported that prospective students in their 30s were often accompanied by mom or dad at interviews and orientations. And grad school applications of every kind reflected a dramatic rise in the telltale markers of "parental involvement." Funny, you'd think that kids who'd been taking college coursework since puberty would be better prepared for independent living—but no. Faith is required when it comes to this sort of change. Faith and a little tough love.

In Graham's final high school years, I watched as his older friends and teammates went off to colleges no more than an hour away. They would return home on Thursday night, hang out with friends and girlfriends, eat their mom's good cooking, and not return to campus till Monday morning. This was not just in the fall but well into the spring and their sophomore years. Every bone in my body knew this was not the experience of going to college. New ties can't be made till the old ties are broken, and, as a result, these boys were slow to avail themselves of the possibilities college presented. I took their lives as a cautionary tale, saying to Graham more often than he probably needed to hear it, "When you go, you're going. You can come home after a month or so, but you will not be coming back here every weekend."

Lon reminded me that the poor kid was only 16 at the time and that I might be making him feel unloved. I didn't only tell Graham what he couldn't do, but what he needed to do. "You need to stay down in the dorm and get through those first lonely weekends just like everyone else. You need to sit in your room and be bored enough or homesick enough or uncomfortable enough to walk out in the hall and find someone else who's feeling the same way and then go out and order a pizza. This is how a new life begins."

By the time Graham actually left, I didn't need to make the speech. Actually, I wavered slightly, seeing the crimp in Lon's eyes, "Well, give it ten days at least, then we can see if you want to come home for a night." That second weekend Graham's roommate, who was without a car, was determined to make the rounds of the fraternity open houses. He needed Graham to drive him. Graham had no interest, would have preferred to stay in the room and watch Sports Center. His roommate persisted, finally getting my son up and out and into the good new thing. They went to several houses that felt too ruffian, too slick, too jockish. Then they arrived at one that, in Graham's words, felt "just right." In the principle of the sorting hat, he had found his House.

Within a few weeks, he was too busy to even think of coming home. Over the next four years, I watched as the infrastructure that the Greek system provides created an opportunity for abundant socializing with a wide group of people, a chance to do some good in the world under the auspices of philanthropy, a chance to get leadership and planning experience, to wear the mantle of responsibility for one's peers, and to develop a network of alumni on which to rely as they got ready to move on. It didn't hurt that, the year he joined, his House had just come off of a period of sanctions and everyone was on their best behavior.

When I asked him how people characterized the Long Beach chapter of Kappa Sigma, he said without a hint of sarcasm, "We're the gentleman's fraternity." I knew that even my beloved Graham could be as guilty as the next kid of telling his mom what he figured she wanted to hear, but after meeting more than a dozen of his fraternity brothers and sorority sisters, I think he was telling the truth. He has made friends and contacts and a solid foundation of leadership and people skills for life. And I know that none of this would have happened if, in those first hard days of transition, he had still had one pampered foot in his own warm bed.

The showdown at Mount Carmel should have been the last tough love lesson Ahab ever needed. The LORD had won, the rain had returned, the false prophets had all been slaughtered; the stage should have been set for a new and redeemed kingdom of Israel. But Ahab was weak, and

Jezebel was one of the shrewdest lobbyists for evil ever to walk the Middle East. Here's what happened instead:

Ahab was bored. Looking out over his land, he decided—as people without much of a purpose in life tend to do—that he needed more of something to be happy. There was a vineyard right next to the King's palace, a patch of land passed down to a good and godly man named Naboth through a process of ancestral inheritance. Ahab thought that Naboth should give him the land so he could plant a vegetable garden there. Ahab offered to pay him or to give him some other land of greater value, but Naboth refused. This was the land of his father and his grandfather and his great grandfather, and the LORD, he explained, had forbidden the family from releasing it. Naboth was sorry, but he simply could not do what the King was asking.

Ahab returned home sullen and resentful. **"He lay down on his bed, turned away his face, and would not eat."** Actually, the fact that Ahab felt an urge to grow vegetables might have spoken to some nascent goodness in him, however poorly formed. Or perhaps, uncertain when God might punish him again, he thought he'd do a little canning before the next drought. Either way, a good wife would have helped him see the value in Naboth's loyalty to his family land, or suggested another parcel where Ahab could grow his vegetables—they could do it together even, tilling the soil in his-and-hers sun hats—or try to understand what was lacking in his life that he suddenly felt a desire for a peasant's pasttime.

Jezebel had no such goodness in her. Seeing her husband pout, which she found more irritating than sympathetic, she quickly hatched a plan, enlisting her corrupt assembly members to help. A letter is issued with the king's seal calling for a fast—as if to imply they'd be listening for God's will—and a meeting of the assembly. **"Two scoundrels"** were placed opposite Naboth and assigned to accuse him. **"You have cursed God and the King,"** they say for the record, at which point Jezebel gives the order for Naboth to be stoned to death, and his ancestral property given over to her husband.

Some time had passed since any activity on the part of Elijah had been recorded. Upon Naboth's death, the word of the LORD came to him once again, revealing that Ahab was in Naboth's vineyard, and instructing Elijah to deliver this final message: **"Have you killed, and also taken possession? Thus says the LORD: In the place where dogs licked up the blood of Naboth, dogs will also lick up your blood."**

Ahab responded to Elijah, **"Have you found me, O my enemy?"**

"I have found you. Because you have sold yourself to do what is evil in the sight of the LORD. I will bring disaster on you: I will consume you, and will cut off from Ahab every male, bond or free, in Israel ..."

"Also, concerning Jezebel the LORD said, 'The dogs shall eat Jezebel within the bound of Jezreel. Anyone belonging to Ahab who dies in the city the dogs shall eat; and anyone of his who dies in the open country the birds of the air shall eat.'" (1 Kings 21:19-24)

202

Most Americans, even worshipping Christians, are unfamiliar with these stories. Hearing them for the first time, we are inclined to think that God is more like a mobster than a good and loving Lord. But when I consider the resolute culture of self-interest and backroom deals in America's corporate and political systems today, the idea of ivory tower villains dying shamefully and alone feels very much to me like justice. Because a loving God loves the whole of his people, the whole of humanity, and when those in power do not help Him care for the greater good, a correction is needed. Then, and now.

These corrections rarely happen in a timeframe that we find satisfactory. In fact, in the history of the Kingdoms of Israel and Judah, over the almost 500-year span chronicled in 1 & 2 Kings, there are many more evil kings than good ones. There is also a greater concentration of prophetic activity than in any other time in biblical history. Sometimes the LORD speaks through leaders and sometimes through prophets. Sometimes through shepherds, or young boys with good aim, or adolescent girls with willing hearts, or babies born in hay and muck. But always and forever, He speaks.

Why is it necessary to go through these periods when good does not prevail? Well, a biblical interpretation tells us that this is the consequence for our refusal to accept even the smallest of limitations back in the Garden of Eden. Paradise is yours, God said. Peace and harmony and joy and a life free from worry about provision or purpose, all this is yours. With only one stipulation. **"You may freely eat of every tree in the garden; but of the tree of the**

knowledge of good and evil you shall not eat, for in the day that you eat of it you shall die" (Genesis 2:16-17). We just couldn't resist. And as a result, life is harder and messier and much more like death than it was intended to be.

So here we are, short on work, short on hope, overextended yet certain that our children can, should, must do better. We moan "Oh God please don't let them be left behind" but we don't say it on our knees, but rather, at the bookstore where we buy the tomes of practice tests, at the sports practices and drama recitals, at the therapists and the pharmacists and the homeopathic vitamin vendors; we say it as we take out second mortgages to pay for the tutors and the enrichment trips and the young leaders conferences. "Oh God, we cry out, please don't let our children be troubled or poor. Please don't let them hate us if their lives don't work out well. Please don't make us have to provide for them forever if the world can't see how great they are. If the world won't be kind enough to overlook their shortcomings. Oh God," we cry out, in a watered-down, fence-sitting, OMG sort of whine, then rush to the horizon to look for proof of blessings fat as hail.

Remy's CHSPE test results came in last week. She passed the English and the Grammar and the Reading Comprehension with high marks. She got a 4 out of 5 on her essay. She missed the math by the equivalent of one problem. I had a feeling that might happen when she emerged from the test in the final group of kids, reporting that she'd barely been able to finish the math section. Ironically, the math was the thing she was best prepared for, she simply ran out of time. I had wondered about that possibility when I noticed that the practice tests had only 50 reading comprehension questions while the real test would have 80; of all the areas that would require extra time and concentration, that would be it.

But the victories were far greater than the losses. She had gone to a strange place and done really well on a standardized test—this in itself was a first. The test sections she had passed did not need to be repeated. She would retake the math section in the spring, having the entire 3 ½ hours to do it. And above all, the results no longer mattered. We had not waited for the system to decide what was best for her life. We had moved when the Spirit said "Now!"

There is a moment in the experience of giving birth when you feel the urge to push. When I was delivering Graham the urge had come before the timing was just right and I was told to resist. I felt as if a locomotive had been attached to my body at the waist and was attempting to pull me out of the room while I was instructed to stay put. Now, stepping off the runaway train of a standardized life with my daughter was like the final release of that driving force that had hailed the onset of parenthood. I could see the train racing off down the track and my body went weak, a lifetime of striving giving way to a new acceptance. Life at the speed of breath. Life with no other judge but the One who created us.

Do you remember that great scene in the stoner classic "Fast Times at Ridgemont High?" Sean Penn's Spicoli tells Mr. Hand something that the teacher views as frivolous, and Mr. Hand responds by reminding Spicoli about what he will and won't allow on *his* time. "Mr. Hand," Spicoli responds. "I've been thinking. If you're here, and I'm here, then isn't this really *our* time?"

The gift of pulling Remy out of a standardized life was a blessing as much for me as for her. I no longer had to wake up in the dark, worry about what horrendous things she would be asked to do each night for homework, or how I was ever going to ensure she got enough sleep. Free from the constraints of having the world determine what she'd need to know and do and by when, I could let her settle into her own natural rhythms, and begin, like Fannie Farmer, to chart her own course.

Christmas is a month away. If all continues to move forward as it has, I will have finished the first draft of this book. I will have helped set the stage for our new vicar to become our new pastor. And Remy will have already earned her first 3 units of college math credit. She will have read a half dozen books (and no Spark Notes), written an essay a week, discovered a new adult theatre group, studied deeply—and with a biologist's fastidiousness—the habits of her new bearded dragon, and created a tableau of Adam and Eve in the Garden made out of a thousand pencils' worth of shavings; a single black curly-q snakes out above the apple three-dimensionally, the idea of sin at the center of a broken world as natural to her as Creation.

But our greatest accomplishment is that the noise in her head has begun to clear so that God's word might come to her again in prayer.

The sins of the father shall be visited on the children. We don't like this to be true, but it's been claimed by too many divergent sources to ignore. The Greek tragedist Euripedes wrote "the gods visit the sins of the fathers upon the children." The Roman lyricist Horace echoed his sentiment: "For the sins of your fathers you, though guiltless, must suffer." Fifteen hundred years later, Shakespeare would express the same idea in *The Merchant of Venice*, "The sins of the father are to be laid upon the children." But God said it first, way back in Exodus.

"For I the LORD your God am a jealous God, punishing the children for the sin of the fathers for the third and fourth generation of those who hate me..." (Exodus 20:5)

Passages like this make it easy for people to reject the Bible. Who would want to believe in a God like that? But whether we want to admit it or not, sin is serious stuff. If we hate God and reject His commandments, if we choose a life full of covetousness and lies and disregard for others, our children will pay for it, be it by example or God's curse. It seems sort of obvious, doesn't it? How else do kids learn to hate and cheat and scheme? How else do they lose the seed of God that is planted in each heart at birth? How else do they learn to believe that their lives are only as good as they, or their parents, can make them?

207

For me, the thing that redeems this passage—even makes it sort of lovable—is God's admission that he is a jealous God. Jealousy is not the sort of emotion we would expect from the Creator, but then again, this is the Creator who made us in His own image. And are we not jealous people? Do we not ache when our loved ones hurt us? Do we not pine for revenge when those who do wrong seem to be rewarded? Isn't this whole SAT, GPA, Exclusive College obsession, at least in part, about ensuring we won't have to feel jealous at our kids' high school graduations when we hear the good fortune of others, or better, ensuring that they are more likely to feel jealous of us? This emotion of jealousy that God is expressing is very familiar; we all know it. What He's telling us is that he cares for us in the same way we care for those we love—madly, truly, foolishly. He expresses this more clearly in the second half of the passage, which many readers never get to: **"… but showing love to a thousand generations of those who love me and keep my commandments."**

Notice that the reward for loving God is far more generous and long lasting than the punishment for rejecting Him. Then, watch how this truth progresses throughout scripture:

A few hundred years after Elijah's time, God called the prophet Ezekiel—one of the most radical, poetic, and metaphysic writers in the whole Bible (and the transcriber of the earth's first recipe for flourless bread)—and gave him this to say on the subject of the sins of the father:

"What do you mean by repeating this proverb concerning the land of Israel, 'the parents have eaten

**sour grapes, and the children's teeth are set on edge?'
As I live says the Lord GOD, this proverb shall no
more be used by you in Israel. Know that all lives are
mine: the life of the parent as well as the life of the
child is mine: it is only the person who sins that shall
die."** (Ezekiel 18:1-4).

I wonder if the widow to whom Elijah was sent
would have been comforted by this new truth, that the guilt
for her son's illness was his alone. What sins could this
young man have had? And what mother wouldn't gladly
take the consequences herself to spare a child's suffering?
This notion of sickness as curse makes religion feel archaic
to many; so too, the reciprocal belief of prayer and faith
being able to heal. I remember Lon and I talking shortly
after Remy had survived her brain surgery whole and well,
and I had come through the experience changed. He said
that he couldn't believe that God had saved her because
what if she hadn't made it? What if she had died? What
would that mean? That God was punishing us? That there
was no God? He didn't see how he could believe when the
promise seemed so uncertain.

Many feel this way, and it is for them that the story
was made complete, that the Law gave birth to the Gospel,
and that Christ made the final revision on the tenet of the
sins of the father:

**"As Jesus went along, he saw a man blind from
birth. His disciples asked him, 'Rabbi, who sinned,
this man or his parents, that he was born blind?'
'Neither this man nor his parents sinned,' said Jesus,**

'but this happened so that the work of God might be displayed in his life." (1 John 4:8)

Chapter 14

Today is the second Wednesday in Advent, the season in which we attempt to still our hearts amidst the holiday huzzah and prepare a space for the birth of the Son of God. The silence this time of year is unlike any other, richer, more resonant, even without snow. I have a daily Advent devotional that I've used each December for almost a decade now. Today's passage is from a book by Max Picard on my favorite subject, silence.

"The nearness of silence means also the nearness of forgiveness and the nearness of love, for the natural basis of forgiveness and love is silence. It is important that the natural basis should be there, for it means that forgiveness and love do not have first to create the medium in which they appear."

The medium of God, of his love, mercy, and forgiveness, of his joy, hope, and promise, of his power, wisdom and might is silence. This is the medium in which Elijah spent his days, encouraging others to do more of the same. Sometimes the message gets through, even if it seems, on human terms, like too little, too late. And so it was, that after Elijah informed King Ahab that the LORD had decreed that he would be left to the dogs, Ahab was, for the very first time in his life, truly contrite. He **"tore his clothes and put sackcloth over his bare flesh; he fasted, lay in the sackcloth, and went about dejectedly."**

Observing Ahab's behavior—searching his whole heart—God shows himself to be something of a softie. Proudly, He shares his reversal with Elijah: **"Have you seen how Ahab has humbled himself before me? Because he has humbled himself before me, I will not bring the disaster in his days, but in his son's days I will bring the disaster on his house."** (1 Kings 21:27-29)

I would love to offer some sugar-coated wisdom to make this passage more palatable, but I cannot. Bible experts say it is an example of how God is always eager to forgive and quickly responds to a contrite heart—fair enough, got it—but as a parent, I cannot imagine how punishing my children instead of me would be just. But when I finally get to the historic recording of King Ahab's death, I realize that God's first assertion about blood and dogs may have been more revelation than punishment, and that He can make good on even seemingly contradictory promises. Here we see both the restored dignity and the symbolic shame God had promised in Ahab's final hours:

"But a certain man drew his bow and unknowingly struck the king of Israel (Ahab) between the scale armor and the breastplate: so he said to the driver of his chariot, 'Turn around, and carry me out of the battle for I am wounded.'"

"The battle grew hot that day, and the king was propped up in his chariot facing the Arameans, until at

evening he died; the blood from the wound had flowed into the bottom of the chariot. Then about sunset a shout went through the army, 'Every man to his city, and every man to his country!'"

"So the king died, and was brought to Samaria; they buried the king in Samaria. They washed the chariot by the pool of Samaria; the dogs licked up his blood, and the prostitutes washed themselves in it, according to the word of the LORD that he had spoken." (1 Kings 22:34-36)

His son Ahaziah reigned for only two years.

"He did what was evil in the sight of the LORD, and walked in the way of his father and mother ... He served Baal and worshipped him; he provoked the LORD, the God of Israel, to anger, just as his father had done." (1 Kings 22:52-53)

As for a disaster befalling him, it was more of the banana peel on the floor variety. Somehow, upon news that his kingdom was under siege, Ahaziah fell through a latticed window in his upper chamber. His body contorted foolishly, he called for help, sending his messengers to the evil god Baal-zebub to ask if he would recover. With that, the LORD informed Elijah that his work with this family was not yet complete.

Many years ago, when I used to nurse babies and watch Oprah in the afternoons, I would hear her tell her audiences that when God wants our attention he puts a little pebble in our paths, then a rock, then a boulder, then a great big brick wall. And when we keep running into it without managing to learn anything or make any changes, he just keeps crashing us harder and faster until finally we stop and say—"Alright already, I'll try it your way!" This sentiment is expressed five times a day in the opening lines of every Benedictine worship. "Oh LORD come to my aid, Oh God make haste to help me." (Psalm 70:1). Is it possible than even those who commit their lives to the love of God, who live apart from the stresses of the world in settings resonant with silence and prayer, still have their own personal brick walls they need help in yielding to? Evidently. No matter what our circumstances, we must ask for help as readily as we draw breath. For those who stand on the outside of religious life, this seems inconceivable, absurd, pathetic, but I liken it to the knowledge that each of us accrue as we age: only then do we realize how very little we know.

Things might have turned out differently had Ahaziah—laying in a heap of splintered latticework—turned his eyes to the heavens and cried, "Oh LORD come to my aid!" What might have happened to the whole of his family lineage if, in that moment, he had allowed himself to be broken, to recognize the error of his ways, his path, the harm he had no doubt done to many? Who can say for sure how history might have been affected if in that instant he had repented, as his father had done so late in life?

My father died of alcohol-induced cirrhosis at the age of 53. He spent the last several years of his life at a high-end rehabilitation hospital in Pasadena. He died a few weeks before my wedding. His personal effects, which at that point had been reduced to a couple of boxes, included both a simple brass wall cross and a Gideon version of the New Testament & Psalms that he likely found in the drawer of his room. The father I knew did not believe in God, but there in his final days, he had read the Gospel with his whole heart. He had experienced contrition, he had seen the mystery and the grace of revelation and made copious notes in the margins. In the index he had scrawled the names of his oldest friends, his Stanford classmates, beside certain well-known passages with stars and arrows, as if he planned to write to them about the importance of those scriptures to their lives.

Ahaziah never knew of his father's change of heart in his final years. So he cried out to the only thing he was familiar with, his mother's false gods. It was then that the LORD sent Elijah to tell Ahaziah the cost of his looking for salvation in all the wrong places. Elijah spoke first to the king's messengers, demanding that they deliver this word: **"You shall not leave the bed to which you have gone, but you shall surely die."**

Ahaziah, hoping to be able to discredit the message, grills his servants nervously. **"What sort of man was he who came to meet you and told you these things?"** They answered him, **"A hairy man, with a leather belt around his waist."** The king grimaced. **"It is Elijah the Tishbite."** (Can't you just see him biting his knuckle as he says the name of his dastardly nemesis and the organ sounds: dun, dun, dun?)

Ahaziah, planning to apply force to get Elijah to change his prophecy, then sends out a captain with 50 to find him. Elijah is sitting quietly alone on the top of a hill. When the captain says to him: **"Oh man of God, the king says, 'Come down,' Elijah responds 'If I am a man of God, let fire come down from heaven and consume you and your fifty.' Then fire came down from heaven, and consumed him and his fifty."** (2 Kings 1:9-10)

This seems laughable to a modern reader new to scripture, the stuff of fairy tales. But I have seen with my own eyes candles lit in a sanctuary where no flame was anywhere in sight. I have lived through a mysterious fire in our church that left all the original structure intact and the congregation closer than ever. I was rescued from the Bel-Air fire as an infant when all the streets were blockaded off and there was no possible way to get to me, save for the divine, unrelenting love of a mother; I have no doubts about how God works through fire. A strategically-placed bolt of lightning on a scrub-dry hill would consume anything in its path.

But Ahaziah, unmoved by the violent death of his troops, promptly sent out another captain with 50 more men. Moments later, they too were destroyed by the fire of God. I picture Elijah looking off in the distance as the men tumbled flaming down the hill, wondering when—if— they'd ever get it right. This, to me, is the essence of this final story in Elijah's ministry: the story of our repeated attempts, our repeated mistakes, our repeated failure to get right with God. I picture those climbing troops like messengers of our own deepest temptations, marching infomercials of lust or fear or rage calling out to us "More! Bigger! Better! Higher!" and it is only the word of God, the fire and the might of God, that can silence the armies of voices that try to pull us in the wrong direction each day.

Yesterday, I was on the treadmill at the YMCA staring at a silent, close-captioned flat screen of Regis & Kelly. With no sound, I could concentrate purely on the visual; on Kelly, the newer, younger, prettier version of Kathy Lee, and Regis, a 79-year old man, tan, well-dressed, and on top of the world, having his morning coffee and chatting flirtatiously with his TV wife, who is beautiful and tiny and smart and considerably less than half his age. I thought about the message that's being sent into five million homes each day via the seemingly innocuous chit-chat, and couldn't help but wonder if maybe all the talk about SATs and worldly success really boils down to sex: enough money and power, and even an old man can wake up with Kelly Ripa, dump her in a few years and get another one. Kelly, on the other hand, no fool she, has an airtight pre-nup and a promise in writing of bigger and better things, or at least of maintaining the lifestyle to which she has grown accustomed. This is the new Holy Grail of America. This is the message that keeps most couples from ever making it to their 25th wedding anniversary. From missing out on the chance to fall in love all over again in the middle of their lives because they bailed when the first wrinkle or rumple or dry spell kicked in. So now we live in lots of houses and apartments and spread our time and shoes and limited income all over town, stretched beyond measure and knowing that something went wrong, certain it couldn't have been us. We talk about empowerment and wonder which seminar or life coach or psychic to go to next to find

217

it. And all the while Elijah waits, alone on the hill, wondering if the next person who attempts to rise will finally figure it out and humble himself accordingly.

"Again, the king sent the captain of a third fifty with his fifty. So the third captain of fifty went up and came and fell on his knees before Elijah, and entreated him, 'O man of God, please let my life, and the life of these fifty servants of yours, be precious in your sight' ... Then the angel of the LORD said to Elijah, 'Go down with him; do not be afraid of him.'" (2 Kings 1:13-15)

So Elijah went down and delivered the same message directly to the king's face and the king promptly died, as prophesied. But the 50 men on the hill that day had, in the process, learned what it meant to be in the presence of the living God, to humble themselves before Him, to place their lives in His hands, and they would carry that truth with them, returning to their homes and, no doubt, telling their children, and planting the seed of a new good thing for generations to come.

I have always loved Christmas music. Even when I wasn't a Christian, I would turn my ear to the whisper of *O Holy Night* and feel as if the earth was playing its most perfect sound. For many years I didn't connect that tug to church or faith or participating in anything that looked like what the people who bomb abortion clinics believe in. The Christian Family, like all things human, has many embarrassing relatives, to be sure. But when that soaring soprano voice cried out, *"Fall on your knees, oh hear the angel voices..."* there was no human mess that it could not overcome and for as long as the song lasted, I was in my right House.

Later, when faith became real to me, I fell in love with the Christmas ballads "Mary, Did you Know?" and Amy Grant's "Breath of Heaven." Lon would be a little mortified each time he would ride in my car in December and find my Amy Grant cassette; he loved The Cure and Morrissey and anything dark and weird, although he had an unusual affection for the soundtrack to *Jesus Christ Superstar* and many recordings by monks—go figure. Even stranger, Remy, who is the only member of our family who has knowingly and willingly walked in the light of Christ every day of her life, loathes Christmas music. When I asked her how it was possible for a person to love Christ but hate Christmas music, she said she thinks that all the music sounds like the lie about Santa and everything being perfect and happy, and it's just not. When Remy was in 3rd grade, a classmate had told her the truth about Santa, and from that day forward, her life had gotten a lot harder. In an instant she understood that the world, your teachers, your parents could look you right in the eye and lie about some big, red man. In a blink, the illusion of innocence and childhood was gone, and she did not yet have the tools to live in a world that bleak.

Which brings us back to the Garden. What Adam and Eve did was to leap into a new area of awareness before they were ready, and in doing so, ruined everything. They were robbed of their own childhoods. They were forced to tackle evil before they were equipped. It's not hard for me to imagine God spending years with his first man and woman, teaching them, disciplining them, nurturing and loving them and when they were ready to handle more, giving it to them, gladly. Proudly. Here, my beloved children, I have saved the best fruit for last.

When we pressure our children to consider grown-up truths before they have a foundation of safety, love, competence, self-respect, and joy, we damage them beyond measure. It takes a loving parent to protect them until they're ready, even if they're not ready when the world says they should be. This doesn't apply only to SATs and the pressure to succeed right out of the gates, but to sex and appearance and exotic experiences, all things being shoved down younger and younger until there is no childhood left. Kids go from circle time to sexting in the blink of an eye, and those words and pictures can never be erased, not from the websites or their formative minds. They have been, like the hard drives we build our lives on, corrupted for life by a system that teases them into adult behavior long before they have the tools to handle it.

It is our greatest sin, not protecting our children's childhoods. If only we could believe that there is time—that there is a plan and a purpose for them, that they will not be left behind—we might be able to break the cycle of the sins of the father. If only.

Guess what? Elizabeth is now engaged to the lifeguard! I saw her last week at Advent services, riding up on her bike with the wicker basket up front, her white blond hair blowing in the cool, dark Venice night. Turns out her sister is engaged too. I went to congratulate their father, a man who battled a pituitary tumor in the middle of his life and had to cut back for a time on his law practice. He, along with his wife of 41 years—who plays the organ for the church—had provided our sanctuary Christmas tree each year, anonymously donated new hymnals after the fire, hosted our annual sloppy joe suppers, and served in every leadership capacity in the church for going on four decades. He laughed and shook my hand.

"You must be so happy," I said.

With the proudest face I've ever seen, he smiled, "Happy? Are you kidding me? Do you know what weddings cost these days?"

My old friend Cathy died last month. She was only a few years older than me. The last time I saw her was at her husband's funeral; he had died of heart failure at the age of 54. He had been Graham's little league coach during the very best baseball years of our lives. His son, Nick, had been a terrific infielder. Whenever Graham wasn't pitching, he played shortstop, and he and Nick, who played second base, turned more double plays than any 12-year olds in recorded history, or at least that's how it felt to us, to me and to Cathy, as we sat in the stands, shouting and squealing and squeezing each other's knees. Is there any moment more perfect than the double play? It took me a while to wrap my head around the idea that the person who fields the ball is supposed to throw it towards the pocket of air above second base, in full faith that his teammate will be there to catch it.

"But what if he isn't there?" I'd ask Graham.

"You throw it anyway."

"But what if it really doesn't look like he's going to be able to make it?"

"If he doesn't make it, he doesn't make it. But you throw it anyway."

Cathy and David were Jewish, although only she was practicing. There were a lot of Jews on our team, and we used to talk more than most baseball parents do, I imagine, about faith. Maybe it was because it was the age of bar mitzvahs and confirmations. Cathy told me that she had never been inside a church before, that she was told if she walked into a church that the entire congregation would turn and glare at her and shout, if not in words then with their eyes, "Christ Killer!" When I told her we held a Seder at our church, and included the Pentateuch and Psalms in every service, and that our cross on the altar was bare, it was a revelation. At her son Nicky's bar mitzvah, I did not feel that the words or the sentiments were something very different from my own: it was very clear to me that we worshipped the same God, the God of Abraham and Isaac and Jacob, the God of Elijah and Cathy and David, may they rest in peace.

There was another dad on the team, Lou, an overt caricature of a Jew in the mold of Woody Allen. Although his ex father-in-law was a Rabbi, he had no intention of having his son bar mitzvahed. I begged him to reconsider.

"It's not like Christianity, where you can show up later if you want and catch up. With Judaism, if you miss out on Hebrew school, on the chanting of the Torah, and the prayers that need to be recited from memory, you'll be SOL come High Holy Days. Don't rob him of that opportunity to know his culture, his faith."

And so the winning season went, with the North Venice Braves going on to win the entire Tournament of Champions, besting teams from all over the region, with Graham on the mound for the 8-0 win. By the following year, we were all putting on our Saturday best to attend Lou's son's bar mitzvah and bash. I will never forget our conversation about Lou's visit to Rome. He, it seems, had not received the same messages about Jews in church that Cathy had. Somehow, between the cocktail meatballs and the *mazel tov*, our conversation turned to a discussion of Holy Communion.

"Oh yeah," Lou said. "I did that."

"You took communion?" I asked, surprised.

"Yeah, at the Vatican."

"You took Holy Communion at the Vatican?!!"

"What? Is that bad? Everyone was doing it."

I smiled. To me the impulse to know God, no matter in what fashion it appears, is always a good one. The Pope, I know, would have a different take on this. But what I realized in that moment, is how lost we are about the narrative of God in contemporary American culture. Belief is a matter of personal choice, of one's own conversation with his or her Maker, but ignorance of the tenets of faith—one's own and others—is a matter of immaturity. Even as we push our kids to be the masters of all information in the known universe, we ourselves don't even have a kindergarten grasp on the Judeo-Christian story. *The Dictionary of Cultural Literacy*, published over two decades ago warned that "no one in the English speaking world can be considered literate without a basic knowledge of the Bible." Still today, according to the Pew Forum on Religious & Public Life, just over half of American adults can say whether or not The Golden Rule is one of the Ten Commandments (it's not), and fewer than half could name the four Gospel writers (Matthew, Mark, Luke, and John), or the day on which the Jewish Sabbath begins (Friday).

"Now when the LORD was about to take Elijah up to heaven by a whirlwind, Elijah and Elisha were on their way from Gilgal. Elijah said to Elisha, 'Stay here; for the LORD has sent me as far as Bethel.' But Elisha said, 'As the LORD lives, and as you yourself live, I will not leave you.'"

"So they went down to Bethel. The company of prophets who were in Bethel came out to Elisha and said to him, 'Do you know that today the LORD will take your master away from you?' And he said, 'Yes, I know; keep silent.'" (2 Kings 2:1-3)

Chapter 15

"These many beautiful days
cannot be lived again,
but they are compounded
in my own flesh and spirit.
And I take them in full measure
towards whatever lies ahead."
—Daniel Berrigan

On Tuesday night, 11 days before Christmas, I was eating dinner with Graham in the new restaurant that had taken over the old Shakey's where we'd had so many school and sports celebrations over the years. This is when my cell phone rang with the late news about Cathy's death. As I listened to the words—words that never make sense—I stared at the booth across from us, where two young moms—well, actually, not young, but new—sat corralling their clans of tow-headed children clad in tutus and karate whites. I thought about all the days they still had to spend with them, of the days I'd spent with Graham and Remy, and of Cathy's children, Nicky and Sammy, now young men alone in the world with nothing to hold onto but what she and David had made a point to pass on to them. As the psalmist prays, **"Teach us to number our days and recognize how few they are."**

On Wednesday night, I went to church with all the school parents who had come to see their kids in a production of a Christmas play called "Camel Lot." Most of them had no idea what Advent was, all they knew is that their wonderful children were singing *Joy, Joy, Joy* and they could film it and post it, and maybe even for an instant, brush up against the source of it. This would have been my father's 79th birthday, he who had never gotten to meet his grandchildren or see them sing about Joy in this church, but nonetheless knew God before he left this earth.

The next night, I was sitting in a beautiful Temple in West L.A. for a screening of the documentary *Race to Nowhere: The Dark Side of America's Achievement Culture*. Finally a movie that gave voice and audience to so many of the things I felt I'd been battling alone all these years. I was meeting a friend there and, as always, I was early. What a gift those moments were, where in the lobby outside the sanctuary, I was able to look at the folk art-styled mezuzahs and menorahs and the snippets of tapestried Psalms with single words included in the Hebrew that popped out from the passages like a wormhole to the Holy Land. I went from wall to wall, turning wide-eyed like some *shiksa* tourist asking passersby if they could translate. The Hebrew letters danced on the walls and I thought of the girl in the book *Bee Season*, who had learned to make mystical connections to the heart of the universe through letters, through words, through the pulse of the chant of Life.

Over the door to the sanctuary was a passage from Psalms about justice, a concept that the Jewish people focus on more than any of the world's religions. *Tikkun Olam*, "repairing the world," is the phrase they include in their daily prayers to remind them that the world is broken and that justice demands that we help to mend it. It is a shortened version of a longer expression that means, "to perfect the world under God's sovereignty."

To act with justice requires that we consider the needs and rights of all the involved parties. Of late, America has been deeply unjust to its children—to the children of want and the children of plenty. To all children who have been pushed too hard, protected too little, and disciplined too rarely. Even those of us who have raised kids with a faith tradition have often corrupted the healing power of that by buying into many of the same fears about achievement as everyone else.

Fear not. That sure consolation is used over 100 times in the Bible:

"For I am the Lord your God, who takes hold of your right hand and says to you, do not fear; I will help you." (Isaiah 41:13).

"Even though I walk through the valley of the shadow of death, I will fear no evil," (Psalm 23:4).

"Do not be afraid, for behold, I bring you tidings of great joy which will be for all people." (Luke 10:10).

"My peace I leave with you; my peace I give you. I do not give to you as the world gives. Do not let your hearts be troubled and do not be afraid." (John 14:27).

As I sat in the Temple Isaiah, which quickly filled with parents who, from the looks of it, had money and opportunity as well as good hearts, I found myself reading the Temple prayer book. I ran my fingers over the Hebrew letters, imagined drawing closer to the source, considered asking if they'd let me take the book home. Thought better of it. There was a prayer there—not unlike the prayers we read each week in church—that spoke to me of the reasons we were gathered that night. I copied it down in my Moleskine notebook as I waited:

"My God, the soul You have given me is pure. You created it. You shaped it. You breathed it into me, and You protect it within me. I offer thanks to You, Adonai, my God, and God of my ancestors, source of all Creation, Sovereign of all souls. Praised are you, Adonai, in whose hand is every living soul and the breath of humankind."

With that the lights dimmed and together we watched as beautiful, flawed, quirky, gawky, perfect, imperfect young people spoke of their stress and sorrows, of the pressure they felt to be 100% in everything, of the toll it takes on their young psyches, even to the point of suicide. We listened as experts from Harvard and Stanford and the very places that represent the pinnacle of the quest that has led to the troubles, spoke simply and compellingly about the corrosive effects of our current practice of homework overloads, skewed focus on memorization, and intense parental pressure, and the very real prospect that we are creating a generation of kids without any of the tools we'd claim to want them to have: creativity, critical thinking skills, and a sense of passion and joy.

A study of 5000 high school students conducted by the Education Department at Stanford, and documented in the film, revealed that, based on a standard of eight forms of cheating—ranging from copying papers, to plagiarizing, to texting answers—only 3% of children reported never having cheated at all. Many considered the art of cheating to be the primary skill of their academic careers. And there we have it: the end result of focusing on results alone. The entire process is rendered not only destructive, but moot.

In our instant-access technology age, facts are less important than ever. We can Google the date of the Croatian War. We can check Wikipedia for a quick definition of cellular mitosis. But there is no computer that can tell a person what to do when a situation presents deep moral ambiguity, where no templated solution fits the problem at hand, where stakes are high and no one is watching to see how the work is being done. The kids we will want in those rooms will be the ones who know what their Gifts are and how to use them, who have learned them through trial and error, who can tolerate the dark and the silence and the unknown and the clamor, and be still until the rain comes. But those kids are not likely to be the ones in those rooms, lacking the requisite keyword-laden college apps and resumes and CVs. While conventional wisdom dictated they build themselves from the outside in, they never believed a word of it.

In the year before Jesus' birth, which we celebrate on December 25th, a Jewish priest named Zechariah and his wife Elizabeth were suffering deeply. All they ever wanted was a child of their own, but they were getting on in years and they still had not been blessed. God must have forgotten them, or so it seemed. Then, on the day when it was Zechariah's duty at the Temple to enter first and offer incense, an angel appeared to him:

"Do not be afraid, Zechariah, for your prayer has been heard. Your wife Elizabeth will bear you a son, and you will name him John. You will have joy and gladness and many will rejoice at his birth, for he will be great in the sight of the Lord."

"He must never drink wine or strong drink; even before his birth he will be filled with the Holy Spirit. He will turn many of the people of Israel to the Lord their God."

"With the spirit and power of Elijah he will go before him, to turn the hearts of parents to their children, and the disobedient to the wisdom of the righteous, to make ready a people prepared for the Lord." (Luke 1:13-17)

This boy would grow up to become John the Baptist, who prepared the way by preparing hearts for the coming of Jesus, who was, in earthly terms, his cousin. Elizabeth was six-months pregnant when the same angel, Gabriel, came to Mary:

"Do not be afraid, Mary, for you have found favor with God. And now, you will conceive in your womb and bear a son, and you will name him Jesus."

"He will be great, and will be called the Son of the Most High, and the Lord God will give to him the throne of his ancestor David. He will reign over the house of Jacob forever, and of his kingdom there will be no end."

"Mary said to the angel, 'How can this be, since I am a virgin?'" (Luke 1:30-33)

Today the question reads like a punch line, not only for biological reasons but because, in our oversexed More, Sooner, Faster landscape, the notion of finding a 15-year old virgin is, sadly, laughable. But at the time of the annunciation of Christ, there was nothing funny about Mary's question, or Gabriel's answer. He proceeded to explain to her how and why the miracle would happen, assuring her, **"For nothing will be impossible with God."**

Impossibility is the realm of the Divine, is it not? Yet, the possibility of a virgin birth is a stumbling block for many, if not most, modern readers. Personally, I've seen God pull off far greater miracles than that, but I get it—hard truths about X and Y-chromosomes make it tough to opt for a belief in the miraculous. The poet Luci Shaw sheds some light that I find helpful: when Mary asks Gabriel how such a thing could be possible—not unlike the way we ask the same question today—she is really asking God "to

231

widen her imagination, to show her how something so impossible to believe could be so." And so He did.

We don't know much about Mary's parents. They were from the tribe of Judah and were direct descendants of King David. Nazareth, the town Mary grew up in, was home to around 500 people, who were neither rich nor poor, but lived comfortably off the land and raised their children in the conservative Jewish tradition. At night, the families of Nazareth—which would have included the families of both Mary and Joseph—gathered around the fire to recount and enact the great stories of the Jewish faith in Aramaic. This is how Mary, who would not have been taught to read, would learn the Hebrew scriptures and be able to teach them to her son, Jesus.

Mary was the age of most high school freshmen when the angel Gabriel came to her. While our children are juggling smart phones and eyeliner and offers of weed, *Catcher in the Rye* and hand jobs and the PSAT, Mary was preparing to be married to a man named Joseph. When the messenger of God said, **"Rejoice, oh highly favored one,"** Mary was able to draw from a lifetime of scriptural grounding to make sense of what was being asked of her. And it was from that deep well that the answer rose up, **"Let it be with me, according to your word."**

There is nothing that I could ever imagine for Graham or Remy that would be as rich and complex and confounding and rewarding as the plan God has for each of them. Why would I even try? I have not always been as brave and sure as I'd like. I have not always resisted the temptation to believe the numbers, the grades, the narrowness of the gate. But I do believe with my whole heart that nothing is impossible with God. And that allows me to endure the times in their lives when the world wants to tell them that they do not measure up. And to give thanks for the times in their lives when they shine beyond all measure.

My friend Kate Campbell came through town just before Christmas. She put on a concert at our little church school and a private one in our home. She stood in the corner where the Christmas tree is now in its full finery and sung about all the strange and wonderful ways mystery weaves itself through people's lives. I had only one song request, which she played for us that night. I played it again at the monastery retreat that weekend, and every single day in my car as I wrote this book, showing up at my desk each morning to see which new pieces of the puzzle God would drop in my lap. Kate's arrangement of the Prayer of Thomas Merton is, for me, the soundtrack of this book. And it goes like this:

"My Lord God,
I have no idea where I am going,
I do not see the road ahead of me.
I cannot know for certain where it will end.
Nor do I really know myself,
and the fact that I think
I am following Your will
does not mean that I am actually doing so.

But I believe that the desire to please you
does in fact please you.
And I hope that I have that desire
in all that I am doing.
I hope that I will never do
anything apart from that desire.
And I know that if I do this
You will lead me by the right road
though I may know nothing about it.
Therefore will I trust You always
though I may seem to be lost
and in the shadow of death.
I will not fear,
for You are ever with me,
and You will never leave me
to face my perils alone."

When Elijah and Elisha and 50 of the LORD's prophets arrived at the Jordan River, Elijah took his mantle, rolled it up, struck the water, and the water parted, just as it had for Moses. Only Elisha and his mentor crossed to the other side, and in what they both knew would be their final moment together, Elijah asked Elisha what he could do for him.

"'Please let me inherit a double share of your spirit,' Elisha asked. 'You have asked a hard thing: yet, if you see me as I am being taken from you, it will be granted you; if not, it will not.'"

"As they continued walking and talking, a chariot of fire and horses of fire separated the two of them, and Elijah ascended in a whirlwind into heaven."

"Elisha kept watching and cried out, 'Father, father! The chariots of Israel and its horsemen!' But when he could no longer see him he grasped his own clothes and tore them in two pieces."

"He picked up the mantle of Elijah that had fallen from him, and went back and stood on the bank of the Jordan." (2 Kings 2:9-13)

When he struck the water with Elijah's mantle he said, **"Where is the LORD, the God of Elijah?"** and the water parted and Elisha went back over to join the company of prophets, who bowed down on the ground just as the Wise Men and the shepherds would do nearly 900 years later, in a stable in Bethlehem, where the mantle had been passed once more, and the Word of God had become flesh and dared to live among us.

My reading glasses just broke. Not just any pair, but the very first pair I ever bought, the ones I use exclusively for my writing and my morning devotional reading. Other pairs are scattered all over the house for reading the news or the knobs on the stereo, but not these. These are for Holy Work. And now they are broken. And the book is nearly done. His timing is not our timing and His ways are not our ways. And I will rejoice and be glad.

The rain has finally come. After the coldest summer and the hottest fall on record, there is finally rain and cold and the weather of introspection that befits this sacred season. The last candles on the menorahs have been snuffed out, the last plates cleared from the gatherings of the Jewish faithful where many among them still save a chair for Elijah. The fourth candle on the Advent wreaths of the Christian faithful will be lit this weekend as we prepare for the celebration of the birth of Jesus and recognize the earthly mother who made it possible. The torch is passed from Moses to Christ, from Elijah to Mary, as we honor the spirit of those who, with trembling hearts and unimaginable consequences, acted humbly and fearlessly to do that which God had set before them. Daily they prayed. Daily they listened. Daily they obeyed—or tried to. In the end, they became larger than life by simply living the lives that God had prepared for them. No more, no less.

There is an old Hasidic saying I love: "Everyone should carefully observe which way his Heart draws him and then choose that way with all his strength." These observations cannot be made by others. They are the private conversations conducted in the hearts of the children of God of all ages listening for His will for them. In the spirit of Elijah, Christ spells out God's promise of a plan and a place for each one of us:

"In my Father's house there are many rooms. If it were not so, would I have told you that I go to prepare a place for you? And if I go and prepare a place

for you, I will come again and will take you to myself, so that where I am, you may be also." (John 14:2-4)

On New Year's Eve, Remy and I were driving home from skate practice. As always, she kept her eyes peeled for the homeless huddled on street corners, in alleys. It was no longer raining but cold, at least by L.A. standards.

"You know what I think would make them feel better, Mom?" Remy chimed. "Some nice warm cake."

I thought of Elijah's angel and smiled. "Yes, I bet that would make them feel better."

We pulled into the corner store to pick out the cake mix and the frosting and the sprinkles and, all the next day, while the nation turned its attention to parade floats and football games, Remy baked cupcakes. She frosted them with care and decorated each one as if it were a Valentine for her beloved. While they were still warm, we put them on trays and drove around the neighborhood. You didn't have to go far to find the homeless; they were every few blocks throughout Venice and Mar Vista and Culver City.

"There," Remy said, pointing. And then, to me, as I pulled the car over. "Stay here. Don't watch."

I looked in the rearview mirror as she approached the man covered in soiled blankets. Saw her place a cupcake, then another, in his filthy, outreached hands. She smiled ebulliently as she returned to the car with her tray, set it in the back seat, reached for the Purell. We drove around for three hours until all the cupcakes were gone, leaving some alongside sleeping mounds—a surprise treat for when they

237

woke up. Only one man refused. Remy left a cake on a newsstand beside him anyway.

"I could tell he was just being stubborn," she said, grinning. "Like me."

"The glory of God
is a human being fully alive."
Irenaeus, 2nd-century bishop

I finished the second draft of this book in early February, the day before Remy's 17th birthday. She passed her CHSPE a few weeks later and enrolled in her first classes at Santa Monica College. That same month I was elected President of the congregation of First Lutheran Church of Venice, the place where I'd first come to faith 17 years before. The place where I had learned what it meant to be a member of the Body of Christ, each with his own gifts, all connected in and under and through the shared love and mercy of God's gift to us, his Son.

Throughout the month, I endeavored to catch up on all the housework I'd been overlooking—an occupational hazard. Rummaging through my bathroom drawers, I came across an old velvet box with a charm I didn't even remember having. It was a flat 14K gold square embossed with a gavel on it, and on the back—oh my gosh, I remember now.

The charm was a gift from my dad when I was at Marlborough, an impossibly selective all-girls private 7-12 school in L.A. Before I even turned it over, I knew what it would say. *President, 7th Grade.* I rubbed the charm between my fingers and set it on the ledge of my bathroom mirror so as never to forget again.

And I know that my Father in heaven is smiling.

ABOUT THE AUTHOR

Heather Choate Davis began her writing career as an advertising copywriter. Over the past 30 years, she's written screenplays, teleplays, one-acts, liturgies, and books, taught creative writing and Junior Great Books, created an original, arts-based vespers called The Renaissance Service™, and led retreats at a high desert monastery. She has an MA in Theology from Concordia University, Irvine and is the co-founder of icktank. She lives in Mar Vista, CA with her husband, Lon. You can find her at heatherchoatedavis.com, and follow her on Facebook for news of upcoming books and talks.

OTHER TITLES BY
HEATHER CHOATE DAVIS

Baptism by Fire:
The true story of a mother who finds faith
during her daughter's darkest hour

The Pitcher's Mom

Man Turned in on Himself:
Understanding Sin
in 21st-Century America

Loaded Words:
Freeing 12 Hard Bible Words from their Baggage
(co-authored)

happy are those:
ancient wisdom for modern life

Made in the USA
Lexington, KY
06 September 2019